# The Aims
## of
# Interpretation

E. D. Hirsch, Jr.

The University of Chicago Press

*Chicago and London*

For
Eric, John, Ted, and Elizabeth

The University of Chicago Press, Chicago 60637
The University of Chicago Press, Ltd., London

© 1976 by The University of Chicago
All rights reserved. Published 1976
Phoenix Edition 1978
Printed in the United States of America

86 85 84 83 82 81 80     5 4 3

*Library of Congress Cataloging in Publication Data*

Hirsch, Eric Donald.
  The aims of interpretation.

  Includes index.
  1. Hermeneutics.   I. Title.
PN81.H49        220.6′3         75-21269
ISBN: 0-226-34241-7 pbk.

# Contents

*Acknowledgments*                                                      v

1. Introduction: Meaning and Significance                              1

**Part One: Current Issues in Theory of Interpretation**

2. Old and New in Hermeneutics                                        17
3. Faulty Perspectives                                                36
4. Stylistics and Synonymity                                          50
5. Three Dimensions of Hermeneutics                                   74

**Part Two: The Valuative Dimension**

6. Evaluation as Knowledge                                            95
7. Privileged Criteria in Evaluation                                 110
8. Some Aims of Criticism                                            124
9. Afterword: Knowledge and Value                                    146

*Notes*                                                              159
*Index*                                                              171

# Acknowledgments

Chapters of this book contain materials first published elsewhere. Chapter 2, "Old and New in Hermeneutics," appeared in a special issue of *The Journal of Religion* (July 1975) where it was titled "Current Issues in Theory of Interpretation." Portions of chapter 3, "Faulty Perspectives," have appeared in *Lebendige Form*, edited by J. L. Sammons and E. Schürer (Munich: Fink Verlag, 1970), and in *Essays in Criticism*, vol. 25 (January 1975). Chapter 4, "Stylistics and Synonymity," first appeared in *Critical Inquiry*, vol. 1 (March 1975). Chapter 5, "Three Dimensions of Hermeneutics," is slightly changed from its first appearance in *New Literary History*, vol. 3 (Winter 1972). Chapter 6, "Evaluation as Knowledge," first appeared in *Contemporary Literature*, vol. 9 (Summer 1968). Chapter 7, "Privileged Criteria in Evaluation," first appeared in *Problems of Literary Evaluation*, edited by J. Strelka (University Park: Pennsylvania State University Press, 1969). Chapter 8, "Some Aims of Criticism," contains material previously published in *Literary Theory and Structure: Essays in Honor of William K. Wimsatt*, edited by F. Brady, J. Palmer, and M. Price (New Haven: Yale University Press, 1973), and also material first published in *College English*, vol. 36 (December 1974). Chapter 9, "Afterword," contains some material first published in *Daedalus*, vol. 99 (Spring 1970). I wish to thank the several editors and publishers for courteously permitting me to reprint these materials.

Earlier drafts of several chapters were read as lectures, and among my hosts for these lectures I wish to single out for particular thanks the Center for the Humanities of Wesleyan University for giving me an opportunity in 1973 to write and present a version of chapter 2 under the auspices of the Center.

I owe a great deal to friends and colleagues who have commented on the ideas of the book. I am especially indebted to Wayne Booth for reading the first, inchoate version, and making valuable suggestions for improving the manuscript.

# 1
# Introduction:
# Meaning and Significance

Except for this chapter and the final one, the chapters that follow are self-contained essays originally contributed to festschriften and journals, or presented as lectures, but always conceived as parts of a coherent book. At the center of the envisioned book, as I first imagined it some years ago, was the subject of literary evaluation—a topic I had not developed very fully in my previous theoretical work. But in the course of time another sort of subject connected with theory of interpretation also presented itself insistently to my mind, and I gradually began to foresee a book that fell into two related parts, corresponding roughly to the distinction in hermeneutics between meaning and significance. Meaning and its relation to valid interpretation had been the central subject of my earlier work; the central subject of this book was at first to be significance and its relation to literary evaluation. But the plan was only half fulfilled. My further speculations on the subject of meaning turned out to be just as compelling as my ideas on evaluation, so that the present book divides itself into two almost equal parts. The unifying theme that binds these two parts together is the defense of the possibility of knowledge in interpretation. At every point, the stable determinacy of meaning is being defended, even when significance is under discussion, for without the stable determinacy of meaning there can be no knowledge in interpretation, nor any knowledge in the many humanistic disciplines based upon textual interpretation. In order to enhance the already implicit coherence of the chapters, I have made revisions in the original essays by adding new materials, deleting some repetitive passages and inserting some cross-references.

The concepts governing the two parts of the book, meaning

and significance respectively, are applications to theory of interpretation of a quite general epistemological distinction. I first
encountered the distinction, as I remember, in Husserl's illuminating book, *Erfahrung und Urteil,* expressed by him as the
"inner and outer horizons" of any act of knowing. This distinction has been central to my thinking and writing on hermeneutic
theory since 1960, when I devoted a section of an essay to
meaning and significance under the heading "The Two Horizons
of Textual Meaning."[1] I develop this distinction further in the
present book, pages 79–81. I believe that the concepts of meaning and significance, or of any analogous distinctions, are essential concepts for comprehending how meaning could be stable
and determinate, and hence how interpretive knowledge is possible. Recently, in a quite unexpected quarter, I discovered an
unsuspected ally fostering this hermeneutical distinction. The
following passage is from Lucien Goldmann's essay "Genetic
Structuralist Method in the History of Literature":

> The illumination of a meaningful structure constitutes a pro-
> cess of comprehending it [meaning]; while insertion of it into
> a vaster structure is to explain it [significance]. As an example:
> to throw light on the tragic structure of Pascal's *Pensées*
> and Racine's theater is a process of comprehending them;
> inserting them in extremist Jansenism while setting forth the
> structure of the latter is a process of comprehending the latter,
> but is a process of explaining the writings of Pascal and
> Racine; inserting extremist Jansenism into the global history of
> Jansenism is to explain the first and comprehend the second.
> To insert Jansenism, as an ideologically expressive movement,
> into the history of the nobility of the robe of the seventeenth
> century is to explain Jansenism and to comprehend the nobil-
> ity of the robe.[2]

It should be obvious from Goldmann's account that such a
distinction is potentially applicable to any act of attention whatever, and to any text or part of a text. In the present book, unless
otherwise specified, the term "meaning" refers to the whole
verbal meaning of a text, and "significance" to textual meaning
in relation to a larger context, i.e., another mind, another era, a

wider subject matter, an alien system of values, and so on. In other words, "significance" is textual meaning as related to some context, indeed any context, beyond itself.

Recently I have come to understand more clearly than I did just why this distinction—crucial to the determinacy and stability of meaning and hence to the possibility of hermeneutical knowledge—has been the main bone of contention for critics of my earlier book, particularly for those relativists who deny the possibility of hermeneutical knowledge. These dogmatic relativists, whom I call cognitive atheists, insist strongly upon the artificiality of any distinction between meaning and significance. I have noticed that resistance to my theories has usually manifested itself as resistance to this distinction. I believe it is not the distinction itself, however, but rather what it entails regarding dogmatic relativism that lies behind this resistance. For the distinction itself is far from artificial; it is natural and universal in our experience. In fact, if we could not distinguish a content of consciousness from its contexts, we could not know any object at all in the world. The context in which something is known is always a different context on a different occasion. Without actualizing such distinctions, we could not recognize today that which we experienced yesterday: this inkwell, that phonograph recording, for such re-cognition entails an ability to demarcate a content from its changed context. An experienced sameness of a content (or object) despite the differentness of the context in which we know it, proves real the distinction between an object of knowledge and the context in which it is known. Those who proclaim these acts of re-cognition to be artificial or illusory do not in fact live by their more "natural" relativistic theory of knowledge. Nobody could live by it in his ordinary intercourse with the world, and indeed we learn to live in the world, as Piaget has shown, precisely by overcoming our infantile confusions of content and context.[3] No, the resistance to a distinction between meaning and significance or its analogues, is not a return to a tough-minded, Heraclitean sense of reality; it is, rather, an abstract consequence of a previously assumed psychological or historical relativism. Resistance to the distinction is based on no decisive experience, but rather on a relativistic theory about the nature of experience in general.

It is important to understand that both parties to this theoretical debate are relativists in one sense of the term. Being post-Kantians, both parties accept the principle that any experience, and of course any experience of textual meaning, is relative to mind. Objects *for us* are the only objects we have. But this more general Kantian relativism is in principle quite neutral on the subject of cognitive atheism in hermeneutics; it implies absolutely nothing about the validity of the distinction between meaning and significance. For even if, as both parties accept, contents for us are correlative to our minds, that hardly entails that a change in some aspects of our minds compels a change in all the contents or meanings we experience. Hence the debate is between two kinds of Kantian relativists.

That point is brought into stark relief by the disagreement between two important post-Kantian philosophers, Husserl and his student Heidegger. It was the central disagreement between them, over which they finally parted company, with Heidegger renouncing claim to the Kantian term "phenomenology," in deference to the respected master to whom he dedicated *Sein und Zeit*. Their disagreement, which I shall now sketch in the briefest schematic terms, stands as a paradigm for (as well as an important historical origin behind) the subsequent quarrels of their epigones. In making this brief allusion to their complex differences, my aim is not historical accuracy, since both philosophers changed their thinking over their careers. The historical disagreement is a convenient way of defining the main theoretical issue as simply and clearly as possible.[4]

In his attempt to find a nonpsychologistic explanation for the existence of stable objects of knowledge, Husserl posited a number of functions in our minds which permitted psychology to overcome psychologism. He posited the mental function of intentionality, and he posited the mind's capacity to "bracket" a domain of experience so that the domain could be contemplated over time. "Bracketing," then, is a simplified, visual metaphor for our ability to demarcate not only a content but also the mental acts by which we attend to that content, apart from the rest of our experience. This demarcation, corresponding to the distinction between meaning and significance, alone assures the potential sameness of objects in experience over time.

For Heidegger, Husserl's ideas pertaining to bracketing suggested an excessively abstract cognitive model that left out of account the fullness of the experienced life through which we know something in the world. So in place of brackets, Heidegger took as his model a more expansive epistemic form: the circle, the hermeneutic circle as expounded by Dilthey. The two forms or models are for Heidegger quite antithetical in their implications. The hermeneutic circle is based on the paradox that we must know the whole in a general way *before* we know a part, since the nature of the part as such is determined by its function in the larger whole. Of course, since we can know a whole only through its parts, the process of interpretation is a circle. Experience as we interpret it must, by the compulsion of logic, follow this circular pattern. But since we must in some sense pre-know a whole before we know a part, every experience is pre-constituted by the whole context in which it is experienced. On this model, it is *impossible* to bracket off one part of experience and separate it from the whole of experienced life. What we know at any time is "pre-conceptually" known and constituted by the whole of our world, and since that world changes in time, so must the objects (for us) change which that world pre-constitutes. The "artificial" brackets have been swept away, and replaced with the fulness of lived experience.

Or so Heideggerians and other dogmatic relativists believe. My own opinion is that both parties can be criticized for taking too literally or too consistently these cognitive metaphors, as though they were true and necessary simulacra of experience. I believe that both models can at different times describe different experiences. Neither is a necessary feature of cognitive life, if ordinary experience should be allowed to intrude into these realms. It is not clear to me why accepting the validity in some experiences of the circular, hermeneutical model, should entail its being valid for all experiences. And the Husserlians on their

side readily concede that bracketing is a possibility, not a
requirement of all experience. Their more modest claim seems a
more plausible claim to me. Whenever I am told by a Heideggerian that I have misunderstood Heidegger, my still unrebutted
response is that I will readily (if uneasily) concede that point,
since the concession in itself implies a more important point,
namely, that Heidegger's text *can* be interpreted correctly, and
has been so interpreted by my accuser. Since the accusation
assumes the determinateness and stability of Heidegger's meaning, *and* the possibility of its being correctly interpreted, I admit
the practical error for the sake of the theoretical truth. I was
once told by a theorist who denied the possibility of correct
interpretation that I had not interpreted his writings correctly.

If one had, then, to choose a hermeneutical model it should
hardly be one that entirely excluded the possibility of Husserl's
brackets. The brackets implied by the terms "meaning" and
"significance" do in fact represent something that most of us
believe we experience in verbal discourse, namely, an alien
meaning, something meant by an implied author or speaker who
is not ourselves. Whenever we have posited another person's
meaning, we have bracketed a region of our own experience as
being that of another person. This paradox of self and other in
verbal discourse is even easier to accept (because more widely
experienced) than the paradox of part and whole in the hermeneutic circle. No doubt the paradoxical doubling of personality
involved in verbal intercourse is a bracketing experience for
which some persons have greater talents than others, but it is
nonetheless a widespread experience. The hermeneutic circle, on
the other hand, as I shall point out at the end of the next chapter,
has now been shown to be an inadequate model for what
actually happens in the interpretation of speech. The magic circle
is breakable.

Before I outline the general argument of the essays that are to
follow, it may be useful to some readers if I give an account of
the relations between the present book and my previous one on
the same general subject, *Validity in Interpretation* (New Haven:

Yale University Press, 1967). One purpose of this book is to amplify important subjects that were dealt with only briefly in the earlier one. Over the past few years, when these amplifications have been presented as lectures, they have sometimes given rise to the impression that they constitute revisions of the earlier argument. I do not object to revising my earlier views and would welcome the chance to recant some of them: recantation is such a rare occurrence in theoretical discussions that it has a certain appeal as a proof of one's reasonableness and bona fides. Nonetheless, these essays do not, in any respect that I am aware of, represent substantive revisions of the earlier argument. On this score, I wish especially to avoid some confusions that arose when chapter 5 of this book was published as a separate essay. There I concede that authorial intention is not the only possible norm for interpretation, though it is the only practical norm for a cognitive discipline of interpretation. The choice of an interpretive norm is not required by the "nature of the text," but, being a choice, belongs to the domain of ethics rather than the domain of ontology. This observation had been made in the earlier book, but so briefly that it was generally overlooked by readers:

> The object of interpretation is precisely that which cannot be defined by the ontological status of a text, since the distinguishing characteristic of a text is that from it not just one but many disparate complexes of meaning can be construed. Only by ignoring this fact can a theorist attempt to erect a normative principle out of a neutral and variable state of affairs—a fallacy that seems endemic to discussions of hermeneutics. Bluntly, no necessity requires the object of interpretation to be determinate or indeterminate, changing or unchanging. On the contrary, the object of interpretation is no automatic given, but a task that the interpreter sets himself. *He* decides what he wants to actualize and what purpose his actualization should achieve.[5]

The amplification of this point in chapter 5 does not in the least alter the defense of the authorial norm in the earlier book, though some readers sympathetic to that defense have expressed their disappointment at my apparent retreat, while others have found comfort in the apparent theoretical license to disregard authorial intention. Neither response is warranted. The discussion changes nothing in the earlier argument. Meanings that are actualized by a reader are of course the reader's meanings—generated by him. Whether they are also meanings intended by an author cannot be determined with absolute certainty, and the reader is in fact free to choose whether or not he will *try* to make his actualized meanings congruent with the author's intended ones. No one disputes that a reader can *try* to realize the author's intended meaning. The two important questions are: (1) whether he should try, and (2) whether he could succeed if he did try. In this book, as in the previous one, my emphatic answer to both questions is yes. The reader should try to reconstruct authorial meaning, and he can in principle succeed in his attempt. The amplifications conducted in chapter 5 are concerned with the first question, the ethical one, which asks whether authorial intention *should* be the norm of interpretation.

A second confusion has sometimes arisen over my use of the word "meaning." My emphasis on the determinacy of meaning has perhaps misled some readers into conceiving it to be far less capacious than it is. "Meaning" is not restricted to conceptual meaning. It is not even restricted to mental "content," since, on my description, it embraces not only any content of mind represented by written speech but also the affects and values that are necessarily correlative to such a content. Defined in Husserl's terms, "meaning" embraces not only intentional objects but also the species of intentional acts which sponsor those intentional objects. In the later chapters of the earlier book, my exposition sometimes took a shortcut when it discussed meaning as an object or content. This is a convenience that I continue to exploit in the present book, but the reader should understand that an intentional object cannot be dissevered from a species of intentional act, that subjective feeling, tone, mood, and value, are constitutive of meaning in its fullest sense. One cannot *have* a meaning without having its necessarily correlative affect or value. This point is developed more fully in chapter 6, where I discuss the necessary correlation of value-stance and content. That correlation is a model for all the other correlations of affect and content, act and object, embraced by the word "meaning."

The four chapters of Part I are arranged to form a conceptual double funnel, with the narrow parts in the middle and the broad ones at the two ends. The two general essays, chapters 2 and 5, serve to contextualize and introduce the essays that follow them, chapter 5 being both an introduction to Part II and a coda to Part I. The first of these general chapters, chapter 2, "Old and New in Hermeneutics," describes a recurrent debate between what might be called the legal and the biblical traditions in hermeneutic theory. This general essay had its origin in an attempt, which I soon abandoned, to write a historical encyclopedia article on interpretation in which the recurring issues were to be analyzed in a-historical, theoretical terms. In my early efforts, the historical and analytical aims were so incompatible that I resigned my commission and set upon the more congenial, analytical project of distinguishing schematically some of the perennial positions in hermeneutics. The purpose of schematizing the old debates is to clarify the current ones. The chapter concludes with what I conceive to be its main contribution to the subject—a resolution of some of the old conflicts by the simple expedient of abandoning the hermeneutic circle as the model of interpretation. In its place I suggest a more refined model that conforms with the results of psychological and psycholinguistic research. This alternative description of the understanding process brings the theoretical model closer to experience, and explains in principle why the so-called circle of understanding is breakable. The alternative description is therefore a potentially decisive argument against that form of dogmatic relativism which is based on the model of the hermeneutic circle.

Chapter 3, "Faulty Perspectives," is a tactical sortie against relativism from another quarter. It points to fundamental inadequacies in the metaphor of visual perspective when that metaphor is used, as it so often is, as a model for the process of interpretation. When it is so used, the metaphor is just another version of the naive, entrapped sort of Kantianism implied by the unbreakable hermeneutic circle. I show that most of the assumptions implied by the metaphor of perspective are both philosophically naive and empirically untrue. This argument is carried into those domains, subjective, historical, and methodological, where the metaphor is used to sanction relativism, and to proclaim the irreproducibility of original meaning.

Chapter 4, the second of the two more specialized raids on dogmatic skepticism in hermeneutics, focuses on the subject of synonymity. The implications of this discussion branch out in a number of directions. The doctrine that linguistic form compels linguistic meaning is opposed by my account of the unpredictability of the relations between form and meaning in actual speech. Paradoxically, this "indeterminacy" of form and meaning must be argued if the determinacy of meaning is to be accounted for. Those who claim that under linguistic conventions form compels meaning, are forced by necessity to the corollary that textual meaning is indeterminate. For, all agree that several possible conventions can legitimately control any text. Since the operative convention is indeterminate in principle, the meaning that convention compels must be indeterminate in principle. The doctrine that form compels meaning suffers, therefore, all the embarrassments of the strict conventionist theory analyzed critically in chapter 2. Only if form does not compel meaning is synonymity possible. The chapter demonstrates that synonymity is in fact possible, and that on this possibility depends the determinacy of meaning, the emancipation of thought from the prison house of a particular linguistic form, and the possibility of fields of knowledge generally. That is a big return for the small price of dashing the more extravagant aspirations of stylistics to be a reliable method of interpretation.

The final chapter of Part I, "Three Dimensions of Hermeneutics," discriminates those aspects of textual commentary pertaining to meaning from those aspects pertaining to significance. It summarizes the issues involved in choosing a norm for meaning, and it introduces the issues concerning significance, especially evaluative significance. The essay is an overview which bridges

Parts I and II. Its main contribution, already alluded to, is its discrimination of the ethical act involved in choosing a norm for the realization of meaning from a text.

Part II is devoted to evaluation. Its first chapter, chapter 6, "Evaluation as Knowledge," proposes an important exception to the general distinction between evaluation and interpretation. So much recent debate has been devoted to this subject that it seemed important to try to adjudicate the issue. For historical reasons that do not need restating here, some literary theorists, led by René Wellek, have insisted on the inseparability of valuation and interpretation, while others, including Northrop Frye, have insisted on the importance of keeping the whirligig of taste and preference out of literary scholarship. Since one foundation of my own work is the distinction between meaning and significance, I of course stand closer to Frye than to Wellek on the issue. Nonetheless, it seems to me that the terms of the debate have not been sufficiently refined, and that one ought to acknowledge the limited sense in which Wellek is correct. To do so requires an acknowledgment of the necessary correlation between value and meaning in any *construing* of meaning. To get to the nub of that issue it was instructive to go back to fundamentals and to Kant's third critique. As I observed above, this necessary correlation of value-stance and content, act and object, extends to the whole domain of meaning.

Whereas Part I defends the determinacy of authorial meaning and implicitly defends the privileged status of authorial meaning, one of the main objects of Part II is to deny a privileged status to any single kind of significance, and more particularly to the "literary" evaluation of literature. In chapters 7 and 8, I argue that the "essence" of literature is not necessarily aesthetic, and hence aesthetic criticism is not necessarily intrinsic. Moreover, even demonstrably intrinsic evaluation is not inherently privileged evaluation. This negative argument has the positive aim of defending mixed and *ad hoc* value-criteria. In the eighth chapter I accept the challenge of defining the principles of valuation that I adhere to and which I also consider to be the most durable and beneficial principles. On this last point the reader will not find any new revelations. The only novelty in my discussion is in the theoretical explanation why the classical, mixed tradition of evaluation has been (and is destined still to be) the most durable tradition of literary evaluation.

Chapter 8 also takes stock of our present situation in literary study, particularly with respect to evaluation. The recent over-emphasis on aesthetic values in literature has had a restrictive and inhibiting effect on literary criticism and literary study. The aesthetic conception of literature has too rigidly limited the canon of literature and has too narrowly confined the scope of literary study, leaving present-day scholars with little to do that is at once "legitimate" and important. I argue for the legitimacy of several important kinds of inquiry which have recently been excluded from "literary" study; and I argue for an expansion of the literary canon. In the end I make one specific and concrete proposal to my fellow teachers of literature, for enhancing the value of literary study.

In the concluding chapter, I bring together some of the main themes of the book: futility of relativism, the possibility of humanistic knowledge, and the correlations that exist between knowledge and value, not just in interpretation but in the humanities generally. I point out the structural similarities between the old, outmoded forms of humanistic relativism and the most up-to-date new forms, native and imported. I argue in the end that the application of humanistic knowledge is of more value than the application of a *jeu d'esprit* pretending to be knowledge or value.

One purpose of this book, then, is to give encouragement to those who are still willing to entertain the belief that knowledge is possible even in textual interpretation. The book does not claim that knowledge has in fact been achieved in such and such a case, for we cannot know *that* we know. On the other hand, no philosophical or actual barrier precludes either true knowledge or probabilistic knowledge in interpretation. In those circumstances, cognitive agnosticism is intellectually more respectable than cognitive atheism in literary study.

Some of my colleagues are indignant at the present decadence in literary scholarship, with its anti-rationalism, faddism, and extreme relativism. I share their feelings. Scholars are right to feel indignant toward those learned writers who deliberately exploit the institutions of scholarship—even down to its punctilious conventions like footnotes and quotations—to deny the whole point of the institutions of scholarship, to deny, that is, the possibility of knowledge. It is ethically inconsistent to batten on institutions whose very foundations one attacks. It is logically inconsistent to write scholarly books which argue that there is no point in writing scholarly books. For such cognitive atheists, all principles are subject to a universal relativism except relativism itself. But whence comes *its* exemption? What is the sanction, in a world devoid of absolutes, for *its* absoluteness? We are never told. This question, so absurdly simple, yet so embarrassing to relativism, is never answered by even the most brilliant of the cognitive atheists. It is not answered, for instance, by Heidegger's disciple Jacques Derrida, currently the most fashionable of the theologians of cognitive atheism in the domain of literary theory.

The reader will notice that the names attacked in this book are mainly philosophical names like Heidegger and Derrida. They represent philosophical theories, not persons. The book does not pause to describe by personal name the many variations on relativistic themes in contemporary hermeneutics. Sometime in the future I may write a detailed account of current theories. In this book, relativism itself, rather than its individual manifestations, is the object of attack. On this issue there are only two or three fundamental theories; there is not much that is new, or can be new, under the hermeneutical sun.

Part I

# Current Issues
# in Theory of Interpretation

# 2
# Old and New in Hermeneutics

In this book I write as a representative of general hermeneutics. In the history of the subject, the important distinction between local and general hermeneutic theories has served to define the tradition of Schleiermacher over against more narrowly conceived hermeneutical traditions. Within this line of general hermeneutics stemming from Schleiermacher can be found Boeckh, Dilthey, Heidegger, and Gadamer in a direct, unbroken lineage. (Just as Heidegger was a student of Dilthey's, so was Gadamer a student of Heidegger's.) But the tradition is by no means a uniform one. The relativism of Heidegger and Gadamer runs counter to the objectivism of Boeckh and Dilthey, so that my own objectivist views can be considered a throwback to the "genuine" or "authentic" tradition of Schleiermacher.[1] But whether one takes an objectivist or relativist position, certain arguments favoring general hermeneutics over local hermeneutics seem to me very strong.

The principal argument in favor of general hermeneutics runs as follows: An interpretive model or methodology that is not correctly descriptive or normative for all textual interpretation is also not correctly descriptive or normative for smaller groupings of texts. If, for instance, a literary theorist proposed a hermeneutic theory specially applicable to poetry but not to other texts, this specially devised, poetical hermeneutics might appear at first to be more practical and useful than a general theory for the interpreter of poetry, but this appearance would turn out to be delusive. For unless it could be known that the special poetic theory were correctly descriptive and normative for *all* of poetry, it could not be known whether the theory was a reliable guide in interpreting a particular poem. Hence, although the theory might correctly apply to poetry 90 percent of the time, it would not necessarily apply to any particular poem or crux within a poem.

A hermeneutics for poetry would have credentials as a genuine poetic *theory* only if poetry as the object of this hermeneutics could be reliably separated off from other texts by a boundary line and a *specifica differentia*, thus assuring that the poetic theory would have only precisely recognizable exceptions. This has never been done successfully for the family of texts that is called poetry. Nor has any method of interpretation been devised that would always yield correct results for any one "class" of texts. Every example of local hermeneutics known to me, biblical hermeneutics, poetics, or canons of legal construction, exists in the realm of what Bacon called "middle axioms," which is to say the realm of probabilities rather than universals. Local hermeneutics consists of rules of thumb rather than rules. As a system of middle axioms, local hermeneutics can indeed provide models and methods that are reliable most of the time. General hermeneutics lays claim to principles that hold true all of the time in textual interpretation. That is why general hermeneutics is, so far, the only aspect of interpretation that has earned the right to be named a "theory."

Before Schleiermacher introduced the discipline of general hermeneutics, the term "hermeneutics" was used almost exclusively by biblical interpreters, and indeed the name itself suggests a sacred origin, being cognate with Hermes, the messenger of the gods. According to Boeckh, the Greek word *Ermenia* is derived from an older, uncertain root that antedates both the messenger-god and the process of interpreting.[2] It is uncertain, then, whether the god or hermeneutics came first. In any case, Boeckh goes on to say that Hermes is the "mediator between gods and men. He manifests the divine thoughts, translates the infinite into the finite, the divine spirit into sensible appearance. Thus, everything that belongs to the realm of understanding is attributed to him, particularly speech and writing."[3] A similarly sacred association goes with the Latin word *interpretatio*, and indeed the word *interpres*, meaning interpreter or mediator, is a normal epithet for Mercury, the Roman version of Hermes. So much for the origin and meaning of hermeneutics, insofar as it has a current meaning. In the past few years, under Heidegger's spreading influence, the word has become a rather vague, magical talisman, particularly on the Continent.

From very early times the idea of interpretation has combined and, to some extent, confused two functions, the understanding of meaning and the explication of meaning. One of the earliest distinctions in hermeneutics discriminated between these two functions: the *ars intelligendi*, the art of understanding, and the *ars explicandi*, the art of explaining. Obviously, an interpreter must first construe or understand a meaning before he explains it to others. Nevertheless, it is useful to stick to the broad term "interpretation," which fuses the two functions, since they do go together whenever any representation is explicated. To focus on the prior activity, one can simply use the term "understanding."

It will be helpful to make one more preliminary discrimination before going on to give an account of current issues in general hermeneutics. The public side of interpretation—the *ars explicandi*—is obviously not a monolithic enterprise. It includes not only what biblical scholars have named *interpretatio*, but also what they have traditionally called *applicatio* (significance). Interpretation includes both functions whenever it answers both the question, What does this text mean?, and also the question, What use or value does it have: how is its meaning applied to me, to us, to our particular situation? The most obvious example of *applicatio* would be the Sunday sermon that interprets and applies a biblical text, or the legal decision that interprets and applies a law, or the literary essay that describes "what *Huckleberry Finn* means to us, today." The chief direct value of interpretation is found in this *applicatio*, not in pure *interpretatio* alone. Nonetheless, *interpretatio* is an indispensable foundation for an indefinite number of tasks of *applicatio*, which it implicitly precedes just as understanding precedes explanation.

Before Schleiermacher, hermeneutical theorizing was confined almost exclusively to two domains where correct interpretation was a matter of life and death (or Heaven and Hell)—the study

of scripture and the study of law. With a numinous document
like the Constitution or the Bible, the principles and methods of
correct interpretation are as important as they are problematical. And here we encounter a paradox in the history of the
subject. The more important the issue at stake, the less we find
philosophical and theological scaffolding being deployed to support interpretive decisions. It was the practical importance and
concreteness of interpretation that made legal and biblical interpretation very different traditions. Their diverging movement
was toward safe and practical rules of correct construction for
quite different kinds of texts, not toward universal principles for
interpreting all texts. By consequence, the history of the subject
has yielded only a few fundamental premises, and these can be
consolidated into two philosophical camps, one associated with
biblical, the other with legal interpretation. Current issues in
theory of interpretation are mainly the old issues.

The first position could be called intuitionism. It conceives the
text as an occasion for direct spiritual communion with a god or
another person. The words of the text alone do not "contain" the
meaning to be communicated; they institute a spiritual process
which, beginning with the words, ultimately transcends the linguistic medium.[4] Canons of philological evidence and rules of
procedure do not constrain this intersubjective communion, because understanding is not entirely a mediated process, but is
also a direct speaking of spirit to spirit. The authenticity of this
communion is determined less by philological investigation than
by the vigor of inward conviction, the spiritual certainty of
communion. The process is intuitive, because even though it is
mediated at first by words, it is not constrained, in the end, by
their form.

Intuitionism has a venerable tradition. It is probably the
oldest principle of hermeneutics, being associated from the start
with sacred interpretation. The letter killeth, but the spirit giveth
life. But since sometimes only chosen souls have direct access to
the spirit behind the letter, interpretation must be left to priests
who interpret for other men with instituted authority. Or, alter-
natively, since inward conviction is a hallmark of intuitionism,

sacred interpretation belongs to individual communion, not to instituted authority. Intuition can thus lead just as easily to an enforced uniformity of interpretation as to a permissive diversity. It sanctions Catholicism and Protestantism alike. In the secular domain of literary criticism it encourages oracular, priestlike pronouncements on the one side, and rebellious subjective individualism on the other. In that secular realm, oracular tones and subjectivity are two sides of the same coin.

It is obvious that any interpretive disagreements based on intuitive premises can be resolved only by an arbitrary fiat. But such a fiat could compel our assent only if the spiritual authority of the interpreter-priest were widely accepted, as in past times, though rarely in our own. Nowadays this resistance to authority is a practical inconvenience for the intuitionist position, but that does not in itself show the position to be incorrect. In some respects, intuitionism almost certainly is correct. We must grant in its favor, for example, one inescapable fact in the history of textual interpretation, and that is the imperfect congruence of letter and spirit. If the letter itself did perfectly realize the spirit, no problems of interpretation would exist. But the great diversity of interpretations compels us to recognize that the letter must be an imperfect representation of meaning. The intuitionist must therefore be right to insist upon transcending the letter. And how can you transcend the letter except by spiritual communion at a level beyond the letter? The intuitive interpreter sees very well that linguistic interpretation cannot authenticate itself on the linguistic level alone. It is a matter of empirical fact that the same linguistic form can and does sponsor different interpretations; consequently it must also be a matter of empirical fact that interpretation does always transcend the letter in some respect. The crucial question for the intuitionist position (and I shall defer my own answer to the end of this chapter) is whether, when we transcend the letter in interpretation, we do so by a spiritual communion.

The intuitionist, then, is right to see that the same linguistic form can sponsor different meanings. Also implicit in his position, and also right, as I believe, is the corollary that *different* linguistic forms can mean exactly the same thing, that perfect translation is theoretically possible, as is perfect synonymity. To assert that different linguistic forms can mean exactly the same thing is, however, to contradict the basic postulate of stylistics, which is that different linguistic forms must represent, though ever so subtly, different meanings. And this brings me to the second basic or pure position in the history of interpretation, that of _positivism_. Its associations are historically with legal interpretation, particularly in Great Britain, where judges still reach decisions on the principle that a law means exactly what its words "say," neither more nor less. Under positivism, the mystical distinction between the letter and the spirit is repudiated. The interpreter should ignore the ghost in the verbal machine and simply explain how the verbal machine actually functions. If the rules and canons of construction are made precise, and if the tools of linguistic analysis are sharpened and refined, the problems of interpretation will be resolved into operational procedures. Positivism shows itself to be the natural ally of stylistics and linguistics. The spirit killeth, but the letter giveth life.

Hence, for positivism, meaning is an epiphenomenon, a secondary quality of linguistic forms themselves. Positivism assumes a congruence of the signified with the signifier; of that which is represented with the vehicle of its representation. Thence comes the doctrine that style is itself a part of the meaning it represents. In less subtle forms, the positivistic doctrine has been attractive to linguists, information theorists, and designers of translation machines. In up-to-date stylistics, the naive version has been much refined and expanded until the description of a verbal strategy takes into account the entire linguistic context, including the whole implicit code that lies behind the verbal strategy. After such an analysis has been completed, style is seen to reveal a meaning that is coerced by the conventional and public character of language. Stylistics, then, even with its qualifications and refinements, still keeps to that root principle of hermeneutical positivism espoused by the British judge, namely that words speak their own meaning. Within its context, a particular style requires a particular meaning. The letter compelleth the spirit.

Now the inadequacies of positivism are only slightly less obvious than the inadequacies of intuitionism. No doubt positivism is right to insist that there must be some correlation between linguistic form and linguistic meaning, but one difficulty is that linguistic form cannot itself be confidently perceived or described. A practitioner of stylistics cannot show that a text displays one linguistic form instead of another. His description of linguistic form will have already depended in crucial respects on his prior understanding of what the text means. This may sound arbitrarily paradoxical, but consider the character of linguistic form: it consists of what we might vaguely call grammatical relationships—as these might exist under some hypothetically adequate grammar. Yet even under a perfected formal-semantic grammar, the form of a text cannot be described on the basis of its word-sequence alone. For the word-sequence by itself cannot furnish those linguistic relations that exist only after the text has been interpreted in one way rather than another. The intuitionist takes diversity of interpretation for granted, but it is the great embarrassment of stylistics. It may be supposed that stylistics as an enterprise is supposed to assist and confirm interpretation, but in crucial respects stylistics can only exist *ex post facto* to interpretation. For, when the words of a text are interpreted in two different ways (no matter how subtle the differences), they will display two different styles, which is the reason, presumably, why stylistics experts disagree among themselves as much as do the intuitionists.

One very neat and quite general example confounds some of the basic premises of positivism—the example of irony. Possible irony is not a special case, only a particularly telling one (like possible allegory) that exemplifies the potential plurisignificance of all word-sequences. Irony is particularly convenient because its presence or absence changes nothing in the text except its fundamental meaning. In many cases, perhaps in most, it may be possible to find clues that would persuade all sensible readers that a text is ironical. But there are many exceptions to this which fill the pages of learned journals with interpretive controversy. Some critics, for instance, read Blake's *Songs of Innocence* as ironical, and perhaps they are, but this cannot be demonstrated stylistically, since the style of the poetry is different on the two kinds of reading. In other texts, stylistic giveaways that could definitely solve our interpretive problem are absent, since they might defeat the whole purpose of using irony, which is sometimes to make one group of readers understand a different meaning from that understood by another. My favorite historical example of an ironical text that clearly did *not* contain stylistic give-aways is the one that landed Daniel Defoe in the pillory.

After a stylistician had read the vicious anti-dissenting sermons of Dr. Sacheverell, what would he do with the work by his contemporary Defoe, *The Shortest Way with the Dissenters?* He could hardly claim that Defoe's anti-dissenting recommendations were themselves so extreme as to show themselves ironic. Nobody suggests that in the case of Dr. Sacheverell's extreme recommendations. We know, moreover, that Defoe's pamphlet was taken as being quite straightforward by those Church of England activists against whom the pamphlet was directed. There is an anecdote in Oldmixion's *History of England* of 1735 which tells of a bookseller who "having an order from a Fellow of a College in Cambridge for a parcel of books, just at the time of publishing this *Shortest Way*, put up one of them in the bundle, not doubting it would be welcome to his customer, who accordingly thanked him for packing so excellent a treatise up with the rest, it being next to the *Sacred Bible*, and *Holy Comments*, the best book he ever saw." Only later, after it had been discovered that the author of this excellent plan to oppress, banish, and hang the dissenters, was himself a clever dissenter with a clever pen, did the Cambridge don change his view and, in Oldmixion's words, "forbade his bookseller to send him any more pamphlets without particular orders." Of this narration we can say on theoretical grounds alone, *si non e vero, e ben trovato.* And we know that Defoe did indeed mislead for a while some very clever men who were excellent stylists, even if not stylisticians. This, of course, only inflamed the subsequent rage against the pamphlet and against its author, the anonymous ironical dissenter. Parliament ordered the pamphlet to be burned by the common hangman, and issued a proclamation offering the sum of fifty pounds for the discovery of the author, who subsequently spent time in the pillory and in jail. In going over this famous piece by Defoe, I cannot find a single stylistic barrier to a perfectly straightforward interpretation, and the historical evidence constitutes a prima facie case against any stylistician who claims to find such a linguistic barrier.

Although such examples cause serious difficulties, indeed I think insuperable difficulties, for the positivistic position, it would be wrong and even silly to deny that some correlation must exist between the verbal medium and the meaning it represents. At the very least, there must be some array of possible correlations between word-sequence and meaning. This is the justification of positivism. The crucial error of positivism, and it is an empirical, positivistic error, is to assume that a particular linguistic form or style is directly revealed in the text. Moreover, there is a logical error, a direct self-contradiction in the postulate that style compels meaning. For, on the one hand, when we interpret a text in two different ways we must encounter two different styles; to deny this would be to give up the foundational premise of positivism that linguistic form determines linguistic meaning. Yet, if we encounter two different styles for the same word-sequence, as our basic premise has required us to do, then we give up, contravene, and contradict our postulate that linguistic style determines linguistic meaning, for that postulate implies that the linguistic form is prior to meaning. Stylistics cannot have it both ways. So even if we grant that the intuitionist pays too little attention to the coercive power of linguistic form, we have to concede that the positivist claims too much for this coercive force.

What seems to be called for is some compromise between these two extreme and, by themselves, inadequate positions. Such an attempt at compromise can be discovered in the recent discussions of speech-act theory, based on the posthumous writings of J. L. Austin, who introduced into verbal meaning the concept of illocutionary force.[5] Having taken Wittgenstein's point that meaning is use, Austin discusses how the very same word-sequence can have a different meaning by virtue of having a different illocutionary force. Thus, "You are going to London," could have the illocutionary force of an assertion, a command, a request, a question, a complaint, or an ironic comment on the fact that you are headed towards Bristol. Austin confronts the question, how can the wide range of possible meaning-uses of a word-sequence be confined to one meaning rather than another? That is, of course, the key problem and point at issue between the intuitionists and positivists. The intuitionist says that the meaning is finally specified and made definite by a communion with the author's intention. The positivist says that meaning is specified by a refined understanding of linguistic rules and norms. By positing a dimension of the verbal act called illocutionary force, Austin apparently brings the two positions together. He tells the positivist that a force or act beyond the mere locution and its rules is indeed required for a definite meaning. On the other hand, he implicitly tells the intuitionist that the illocutionary acts do not reside in an arbitrary subjective domain, but belong to the convention-system of language, and can be manifested by prefixing certain performatives such as "I argue that," "I promise that," and so on.

I believe it is fair to say that this attempt at mediation has not succeeded in bringing the positivist and intuitionist together. We need only look at the arguments that are taking place within speech-act theory to see that the old polarity has simply reappeared in a new form. On the one side I find writers like John Searle stressing the conventionality and rule-governed character of speech acts.[6] On the other side I find the indomitable H. P. Grice stressing the dependence of meaning on subjective intention—his version of the intuitionist view.[7] That the old polarity should thus reappear is not surprising, for I believe it is impossible to reconcile the positivistic and intuitive positions simply by granting that there must be on the one hand a rule-governed public dimension to language use, and on the other, a private determination of its range and application. The positivist will always want to insist further that this private determination must in the end be governed by publicly available conventions;

otherwise he will have conceded what the intuitionist claims, and he will find himself in the other camp. That is why the split is destined to remain in speech-act theories, as it has remained throughout the history of hermeneutics. A mediation of the truths perceived on both sides requires, I think, a different sort of accommodation.

I have not yet mentioned a third and final position in the history of interpretation. It is a characteristically modern position, for which the most descriptive term would be perspectivism. What it amounts to is skepticism regarding the possibility of correct interpretation. A perspective is a visual metaphor that stresses the differentness of an object when it is looked at from different standpoints. Under this metaphor come both of the chief varieties of modern hermeneutical skepticism—the psychological and the historical.[8] The psychological version says that a text's meaning cannot be the same for me as it is for you, because we look at the text from different subjective standpoints. The historical version proposes the same argument *a fortiori* for interpreters and authors who stand at different points in cultural time and space. Psychologism and historicism are thus quite interchangeable in the pattern of their skepticism and can be treated as a single phenomenon. Both stress that interpretation is relative to the interpreter, and thus imply that all interpretation must in the end be misinterpretation.

This position (and notice how the very word "position" implies the perspectivistic metaphor) is probably not vulnerable to a decisive attack by means of logic, and I cannot see how it could ever be decisively confirmed or disconfirmed by experience. For, how can anybody ever know whether or not he shares a meaning with another person or another culture? On the other hand, the perspectivist position does present itself, dogmatically, as empirical description. It informs me that I do not understand "Twinkle Twinkle Little Star" exactly as you do or as an earlier culture did. But what has authenticated this dogma in the empirical realm?Whether it is true or false must be a question of fact, not a question of metaphysical necessity. By what a priori argument could I deny the very possibility of your understanding

"Twinkle Twinkle Little Star" exactly as I do? Whence comes this certainty of incongruence?

Since perspectivism makes empirical claims about linguistic interpretation, it is reasonable to bring forward some empirical counterevidence regarding a linguistic domain analogous to the interpretation of written documents. It is a well-established doctrine in phonetics that no two persons pronounce identical speech-sounds. The analogy of this doctrine with the psychologistic view that no two persons experience the same meanings is almost total. Just as no two persons have the same private mental history, so no two persons have exactly the same size and configuration of speech organs nor exactly the same combinations of audible frequencies when they speak. This inference is strongly supported by experimental data, so much so, that we can identify voice signatures through the device of the sound spectrograph with more security than we can identify handwriting. Similarly, regional dialectal differences are at least partly analogous to the historicistic discrimination under which no two cultures can share exactly the same meanings.

Still further analogies could be drawn between phonetics and perspectivism, but instead of pausing here to explain why these similarities are not accidental, I shall take what seems to me the crucial next step in pursuing the analogy. Spectrographic, phonetic description remains almost completely useless for linguistic observation unless it is transposed to the phonemic level. Any two speakers of a language make different sounds, often recognizably different ones, and yet they can perceive the different sounds as being linguistically identical, as being the self-same phoneme. Since we are all aware of regional accents, we are not surprised to hear very different noises being made when, say, the pledge of allegiance is recited. Yet we do not doubt that these different noises are representing the same, self-identical words. Nor is it by virtue of some abstraction that we recognize the words as being the same, but rather by virtue of their being absolutely self-identical as words. The phoneme, the word, the phrase, the sentence, the text: these are not abstractions; they are the very realities upon which the perspectivist bases his skepticism. He says that we all understand the same text differently, not pausing to observe how remarkable it is that we should all have the same text, the same words, whether in black letter or in roman, whether spoken by an Englishman or an American.

Here I am suggesting that what we call a phoneme is precisely analogous to what we call a meaning. In fact, this is to put the case far too weakly. A phoneme is itself an instance of meaning. We can go further. Just as different phonetic noises can represent the same phoneme, so can different phonemes represent the same word, and different words the same concept. All these are instances of the representation of meaning, though at different levels.

Within linguistics this phenomenon has been labeled the principle of linguistic asymmetry by Professor Charles Bazell, who has written brilliantly on the subject.[9] It is at least arguable (as we know from Husserl's arguments) that this principle of asymmetry extends far beyond the phonemic and even beyond the linguistic sphere. In linguistic asymmetry, an indefinite number of lower level phenomena can represent a single, self-identical higher level meaning, as in the phonetic level vis-à-vis the phonemic. When this phenomenon of linguistic asymmetry is accommodated to Husserl's more generalized account, it instances a fundamental trait of our consciousness: an indefinite plurality of mental acts, experiences, or contents can refer to a single, self-identical object. For instance, when on one occasion I speak the word "tangerine," I may be thinking of its flavor; on another of its texture and shape; on another of its color. Yet even though I may be attending to those different aspects of a tangerine (or to none of them), I can still be referring to the very same thing: a self-identical object or meaning. Moreover, this asymmetry is reversible. On both of two occasions I may be attending to the flavor of a tangerine, and yet I may mean something rather different when I use the word on these two occasions. In one of the cases the flavor could be my exclusive meaning; in the other my coincidental thinking about flavor could be irrelevant to my meaning.

If we take Husserl's general principle beyond the linguistic sphere into visual perception, it is more obviously applicable; since a physical object that we see is not defined for us by the particular content of our retinal vision, but by what that content means as interpreted by us. If, for instance, we look at a book on a shelf, we normally conceive the object of our perception to be a book, not just the spine of a book; which is remarkable, since we see only the spine, and nothing of the pages or the other outside surfaces. If we then take the book from the shelf and look at its front cover, we still perceive the very same book, feeling no sense of contradiction. When we open the pages, it is still the very same object. Hence the metaphor of perspective would seem to be peculiarly inadequate even as a description of visual perception. Perspectivism does not characterize the visual perception of normal adults. In this connection it is illuminating to quote from Piaget's *The Construction of Reality in the Child*, where he describes and interprets one of his experiments with young children.

Take for example the following problem. The child is presented with a model, about one square meter in size, representing three mountains in relief; he is to reconstruct the different perspectives in which a little doll views them in varying positions that follow a given order. No technical or verbal difficulty impedes the child, for he may simply point with his finger to what the doll sees, or choose from among several pictures showing the possible perspectives. Yet far from representing the various scenes which the doll contemplates from different viewpoints, the child always considers his own perspective as absolute and thus attributes it to the doll without suspecting this confusion. . . . Then, when the child disengages himself from this initial egocentrism and masters the relationships involved in these problems, we witness a totality of transitional phases. To represent to himself space or objects in space is necessarily to reconcile in a single act the different possible perspectives on reality and no longer be satisfied to adopt them successively. . . . Now, if it is possible for the child to imagine himself as occupying several positions at one time, it is obvious that it is rather by representing to himself the perspective of another person and by coordinating it with his

own that he will solve such a problem in concrete reality. . . .
As we have seen, . . . three formative processes are necessary
to the elaboration of object concept: the accommodation of the
organs which makes it possible to foresee the reappearance of
bodies; the coordination of schemata which makes it possible
to endow each of these bodies with a multiplicity of inter-
connected qualities; and the deduction peculiar to sensori-
motor reasoning which makes it possible to understand
displacements of bodies and to reconcile their permanence
with their apparent variations. [10]

Piaget's research traces how we come to understand the stable
self-identity of physical objects, despite great variations in our
perceptual experience of those objects. We do so through schemata, constructed by us, which correspond very closely with
what we call meanings in our linguistic experience. These meanings are not naively perspectival. It is precisely because normal
perception is not directly perspectival that painters had to labor
so hard to learn the rules of perspective. No doubt, a process
similar to that described by Piaget occurs when a child is learning how to use language, for at the simplest level he needs to
discover how big variations in physical sound can come to
represent one self-same verbal sound. For this the child needs to
construct linguistic schemata analogous to the spatial-temporal
schemata through which he perceives self-identical physical objects. Whether or not the details of Piaget's explanations are as
reliable as his experimental results, we have acquired enough
empirical knowledge about both language and perception to
make the skeptical, perspectival dogmas of psychologism and
historicism look at least dubious. And dubiousness is extremely
damaging to a skeptical dogma that by its nature cannot be
proved or disproved by any evidence at all.

My final observations in this chapter will touch on the recent
expansion of hermeneutics to embrace the whole of philosophy
and life, an expansion we owe to Heidegger. Elsewhere I shall
criticize the importation of Heidegger's philosophical views directly into the narrower conception of textual interpretation (See
chapter 5). I point out that these views, being metaphysical,

provide no help in the concrete decisions of interpretation and set no limit on the empirical possibilities of understanding. Metaphysics, whether that of Heidegger or of Schelling, is the night in which all cows are black.

Nonetheless, the Heideggerian expansion of hermeneutics may be useful in ways not originally intended by the relativistic Heideggerian school. Work that is now being pursued in linguistics (especially psycholinguistics), in developmental psychology, in theory of knowledge, in the work of Gombrich in art history, all suggest that linguistic interpretation follows a general pattern which governs our coming to cognitive terms with our world. Hence, I think Heidegger was right to extend the range of hermeneutics beyond the limited domain of man-made representations, since the fundamental character of interpretation is the same in all our cognitive processes. What Heidegger called the priority of pre-understanding is described by developmental psychologists as the primacy of the schema; by Gombrich, in art history, as the primacy of the genre; by cognitive theorists (particularly those concerned with scientific knowledge) as the primacy of the hypothesis.

On this theory, all cognition is analogous to interpretation in being based upon *corrigible schemata*, a useful phrase I take from Piaget. The model of corrigible schemata, which was exemplified in the description of Piaget's experiments, is, I think, a more useful and accurate model than that of the so-called hermeneutic circle. Unlike one's unalterable and inescapable pre-understanding in Heidegger's account of the hermeneutic circle, a schema can be radically altered and corrected. A schema sets up a range of predictions or expectations, which if fulfilled confirms the schema, but if not fulfilled causes us to revise it. That this making-matching, constructive-corrective process inheres in the reception of speech has now been demonstrated by psycholinguists, who have shown, for instance, that expectancies based on some posited schema (say, a word) not only influence the interpretation of phonemes, but can cause them to be radically misinterpreted. Yet the unexpected phoneme can also cause us to revise or correct the word we were expecting. On the level of the phrase, this same point has been argued persuasively by Dwight Bolinger.[11]

Here we have very strong evidence that the most elementary aspects of verbal interpretation follow the same ground rules as our perception and interpretation of the world. Similarly, in the production of speech, the study of hesitation phenomena provides evidence that the same sort of making-matching process characterizes speaking as well as understanding. Our semantic intentions seem to be matched against preformed schemata which we either use as previously formed, or alter to better match our semantic intention.[12]

For theory of interpretation, the potential importance of this psychological-cognitive model is beyond estimate, though, in its ecumenical, nonmetaphysical form, it has received little attention in hermeneutics. In the beginning of this chapter I pointed to long-standing difficulties in the two polar accounts of verbal understanding, the intuitionist and the positivist accounts. Because of the inadequacies of these traditional views, it is tempting to ignore the whole question of the process of understanding. In 1967, I went almost that far when I suggested that we need to put the focus of hermeneutics on the process of validation, since we do not really understand the process of verbal understanding.

I have now come to think that such caution is misplaced. The process of validation is not easily separated from the process of understanding in either theory or practice. The universality of the making-matching process and of corrigible schemata in all domains of language and thought suggests that *the process of understanding is itself a process of validation*. While this idea was implicit in my earlier writing, it has only recently dawned on me in its proper explicitness. It is true that the term validation suggests a public activity, an objective marshaling of evidence in the cause of an interpretive hypothesis. Nonetheless, the private processes of verbal understanding have the same character, even if they are not similarly systematic and public. For that which we are understanding is itself an hypothesis constructed by ourselves, a schema, or genre, or type which provokes expectations that are confirmed by our linguistic experience, or when they are not confirmed, cause us to adjust our hypothesis or schema.

This description of verbal understanding now has a good deal of empirical support. It is a description that overcomes some of the most persistent and annoying difficulties in the older accounts of understanding. The intuitionist is trapped by the fact that communicable language cannot possibly transcend sharable, and therefore public, conventions. If it could, he would not need words at all. But the positivist, who stresses conventions and rules, cannot explain how these same rules can sponsor quite divergent meanings and interpretations. He cannot, for instance, determine through rules whether an utterance is ironic. Verbal understanding is not purely intuitive, then, but it cannot be purely rule-governed either, and it cannot be some arbitrary mixture of the two, as I have shown in discussing speech-act theory. For our intuitions are open to correction, and our rules and conventions are open to change. The traditional views do not account for those two elementary and central facts about interpretative and linguistic change. The intuitionist cannot explain how or why we come to revise an interpretation. The positivist cannot explain how the rules can change, or how we could know that they change. Yet these basic and central facts about language-change are not in the least problematical when understanding is conceived of as a validating, self-correcting process—an active positing of corrigible schemata which we test and modify in the very process of coming to understand an utterance.

In these final remarks I have offered a sketchy account of a very broad subject, but it seems appropriate to end a survey of current issues in hermeneutics on a somewhat tentative and vague, yet optimistic note that looks forward to further inquiry. Possibly, further study will show certain difficulties in describing a general theory of interpretation as a theory of corrigible schemata. Perhaps the ecumenical impulse that brings together psychology, art history, philosophy of science, and epistemology will prove to be merely eclectic, though I am betting it will not. It is very remarkable how widespread is the pattern I have been discussing. No doubt a model is not just the same as a type, nor a type exactly the same as a genre, which in turn is not precisely the same as an hypothesis. And no doubt an hypothesis is not just the same as Husserl's "intentional object," which in turn is not exactly the same as Piaget's "schema," Dilthey's "whole," or Heidegger's "pre-understanding." Yet important features of all these proposals are quite identical in their character and function, and also in their connection with what we call meaning. This encourages me to think that to pursue this line of interdisciplinary inquiry in hermeneutics may turn out to be not just ecumenical but also illuminating.

# 3

# Faulty Perspectives

The main intellectual (and emotional) sanction for dogmatic skepticism in present-day literary theory is its assumption that all "knowledge" is relative. This cognitive atheism, as I call it, is based mainly on the idea that everybody sees literature from his own "angle of vision," and responds emotionally to literature through his own system of values and associations. Individualized in this way, cognitive atheism is straightforward subjectivism. But other closely related forms in literary theory and practice are cultural relativism, historical relativism, and methodological relativism. All exhibit the same structure; all of them make truth and reality relative to a spiritual perspective. That this doctrine of critical relativity should itself be the single doctrine exempt from an otherwise universal skepticism rarely strikes its adherents as a damaging inconsistency, or even a curious paradox. Tough-minded cognitive atheism usually tends to be an emotional given rather than a developed system. But if mere inconsistency is no bar to dogmatic skepticism in literary theory, one might hope nonetheless for a conversion to agnosticism if it could be shown that the doctrine of cognitive relativity is based on premises that are empirically wrong.

## I. The Metaphor of Perspective

Words concerning the changing appearances of an object, when it is seen from different points in space, came to the lexical scene rather late in modern European languages. Perspective-words are not found at all in the lexicons of ancient Greece and Rome. The Orient was apparently more precocious. Evidence from the actual practice of early Chinese painters shows that they understood systematically the distorted appearance of objects when viewed by monocular vision from a single location in space. But in the West, the "laws of perspective," which is to say the systematic distortions of spatially located vision, were not understood until the fifteenth century, the period when painters worked out the principles for representing monocular perspectives on two-dimensional surfaces.

Why did Western painters take so long to discover elemental principles of their illusionist art? The answer is probably to be found in developmental psychology, especially in Piaget's experiments with young children.[1] In learning to interpret the world visually, every child must go through a long, tedious, error-filled process before he learns to compensate for perspective-effects. In going through this learning process, the normal child is, of course, greatly assisted by a built-in perspective-compensator which he possesses at birth: his binocular vision. The child from the start has a double perspective; he constantly looks at the world from two points of view. Because the distance between these two points is a constant, he gradually learns to reinterpret the distortions of a one-eyed view of the world. That is why the "laws of perspective" were so difficult, so unnatural, and so late to be discovered. To learn them meant to unlearn the basic and arduous lessons of childhood, as documented by Piaget. So wayward is this process of deconstruction that early researches into perspective-effects required special devices like the *camera oscura* and the instruments that Dürer depicted in his "Demonstration of Perspective."

It has taken Western culture an even longer time to discover the spiritual analogues to perspective-effects as represented in such metaphors as *viewpoint* (1856), *standpoint* (1836), *mental perspective* (1841), and *attitude* (1837), the dates in parentheses representing the first occasion of such figurative usage recorded in the *New English Dictionary*. If Renaissance painters required the *camera oscura*, the Victorians, in making their spiritual analogue, apparently required Kant.[2] To assume that one's own sense of reality is distorted by one's spiritual location, on the analogy of monocular vision, required the Copernican revolution of the Kantian philosophy.

But the implied relativism in that analogue is a supreme irony,

since the purpose of the critical philosophy was to defend the validity and universality of knowledge, not its dependence on a spiritual perspective. It is not only an irony, it is a total vulgarization
of the great Kantian insight. This chapter is a sketch of some of
these vulgarizations in the domain of hermeneutic theory, and an
argument against their uncritical and facile application.

## II. The Perspective of History
### Three Relativistic Fallacies

It was chiefly Herder in the late eighteenth century who challenged the assumption that the perspective of human nature is
essentially the same in all times and places. Herder's contrary
view of history has been called "historicism" by Meinecke, who
judges it to be "one of the greatest revolutions that Western
thought has experienced."[3] Undoubtedly Meinecke is right. And
one effect of this revolution was to introduce the metaphor of
perspective into the domain of historical description. Not until
historians began to assume that men's perspectives are essentially different in different eras did they begin to write monographs on the Romantic *Zeitgeist* or the Medieval Mind. In various
degrees of sophistication, such perspectival concepts are now the
staple of literary history.

According to Meinecke, the chief feature of historicism "is the
replacing of a generalizing mode of thinking about human phenomena with an individualizing mode of thinking." But Meinecke's description is only partly accurate for modern historicism
(or cultural perspectivism) in its uncritical forms. Literary history
often stresses the individuality of a period without placing a
correspondent stress on discordant individualities within a period. And this is odd, since those who understand the sameness of
individuals within a period do not very often perceive sameness
among individuals across different periods. Meinecke is himself
an historian, a distinguished one, who avoids this inconsistency.
History of any sort, including literary history, he asserts, would
be impossible on the assumption that man's perspective changes

radically in history; and it would be empty if it assumed that human nature remained everywhere the same. Uncritical dogma in either direction deserves to be called a fallacy. It is not, of course, a logical fallacy, only an offense against experience and common sense.

The first historicist fallacy on my list of three I call the fallacy of the inscrutable past, since under it, one regards persons of the past in the way Englishmen in novels used to regard inscrutable Orientals. Literary historians of this style infer from the past a state of mind so different from our own that its texts can be understood only by an initiated few, from whom an act of "historical sympathy" is required to understand a distant era that seems to be populated by beings who might have come from Mars. I will take as illustration the following inferences of Professor Bruno Snell. After an impressive lexical analysis of the *Odyssey* and *Iliad*, Professor Snell concludes that the Greeks of Homer's day possessed no conscious idea of a unified human self; in the Homeric poems he finds no word for such a concept. By the same process of lexical inference he finds that the Greeks possessed no concept of a unified human body. The Homeric poems refer only to parts of the body, never to the whole.[4] Habitually, then, Greeks must have regarded the human body as merely a congeries of parts. I do not deny that Professor Snell could be right, I only assert that it is exceedingly improbable he is right. I doubt that he would have advanced his theories if he had not studied in a tradition which honored the perspectivist fallacy of the inscrutable past.

Snell's book has been influential, but one could not condemn its interesting improbabilities if these and similar ones by literary scholars had not produced a very damaging reaction among present-day theorists. Theorists like Gadamer, for instance, or like Barthes, rightly object to the cultural narcosis induced by such "reconstructions" of the past.[5] But as an antidote, they recommend that we vitalize the inscrutable texts of the past by distorting them to our own perspective. In other words, they accept the fallacy of the inscrutable past as the premise on which

they base their skeptical counterproposal. It is far better to
distort the past in an interesting and relevant way than to distort
and deaden it under the pretense of historical reconstruction.
Hence, both Snell in his historical reconstruction and Gadamer
in his historical vitalization are extreme historicists and perspectivists. They are brothers under the skin. Both assume that the
perspective-ridden meanings of the past are irremediably alien to
us. In the one case we are asked to join in a perspective that
yields a humanity and a reality entirely unlike our own. In the
other case we are advised to ignore such alien reality as irrelevant to our concerns and to construct instead a usable past out
of our own perspective. If we were truly required to choose
between Snell and Gadamer on this point, the ethical preference
would lie with Gadamer, since a useful distortion would be
superior to a useless one. But we are not required to make a
choice based on fallacious premises.

My second fallacy of historicism is the fallacy of the homogeneous past. Obviously, it is often accompanied by the fallacy of
the inscrutable past, as in the case of Snell, who seems to assert
that *all* the Greeks of Homer's day lacked a concept of a unified
human self. Under this fallacy, everybody who composed texts
in the Elizabethan Age, or the Romantic Age, or the Periclean
Age shared in each case a common perspective imposed by their
shared culture. Literary historians who write on this premise are
content to apply it in the following sort of syllogism:

> Medieval Man believed in alchemy.
> Chaucer was a Medieval Man.
> Chaucer believed in alchemy.

The most distinguished exemplar of this monolithic cultural
perspectivism is no doubt D. W. Robertson. Certainly he represents a convenient example, since, like Snell, he exhibits the
fallacy so very purely. Of course the fallacy of the homogeneous
past lies not in its logic, which is quite unassailable, but in the
implausibility of its major premise about the Medieval Mind, or
the Greek Mind, or the Victorian Frame of Mind.

Used critically, such concepts as the Victorian frame of mind are, of course, entirely reasonable. A shared culture does indeed mean a shared spiritual perspective—where the culture and the perspective are shared. Even odd-seeming generalizations about the medieval mind are reasonable tools, so long as they remain tools—heuristic devices that pave the way into another cultural environment. But to assume that *any* cultural environment is homogeneous, even on the very abstract level at which literary history is conducted, is to make an assumption about human communities which experience contradicts.

Finally my third historicistic fallacy. It is the one I wish chiefly to expose. It now lurks behind many a critical bush. It is the fallacy of the homogeneous present-day perspective. Only by accepting this additional fallacy, for example, can Gadamer offer an alternative to Snell. For when Gadamer attacks the "deadness" of pretended historical reconstruction, he assumes a present that has its own peculiar deadness. To whom, for instance, is historical reconstruction dead? Why, to the homogeneous "us." Jan Kott invites "us" to meet Shakespeare, "our contemporary." Roland Barthes invites "us" to meet "our" contemporary, Racine, to make him speak to "us." But this homogeneity in our present perspective is a construction as artificial as any of the despised "reconstructions" of the past. It is entirely false to Herder's genial insight into the great multifariousness of human-being, both past and present—the original insight of historicism in which all its later fallacies are grounded.

In such later theories, then, Herder's insight into the individuality of men and cultures has been vulgarized. A complementary insight by his contemporary Vico has been repudiated. Erich Auerbach has phrased Vico's idea as follows: "The entire development of human history as made by men is potentially contained in the human mind, and may, therefore, by a process of research and re-evocation be understood by men."[6] To say with Herder that men and cultures are often very different from one another is not to deny that a man can understand someone with a perspective very different from his own. Vico's conception, later elaborated by Dilthey, was that men share a common potential to be other than they are.[7] The distance between one

culture and another may not in every instance be bridgeable, but
the same is true between persons who inhabit the same culture.
Cultural perspectivism, of the sort I have been attacking, forgets
that the distance between one historical period and another is a
very small step in comparison to the huge metaphysical gap we
must leap to understand the perspective of another person in any
time or place.

### III. What is an Approach?

Dilthey's psychological model for our potential ability to understand the past is persuasive and balanced. But Dilthey himself
did not always manage to preserve this balance in his writings. It
is mainly to him that we owe the word *Weltanschauung,* that is,
the spiritual perspective of a person or a culture. In the domain
of literary criticism, the critic's *Weltanschauung* is sometimes
called his "approach," a term first used in this perspectival sense
in the twentieth century. The critic's interpretation of literature
depends on his "approach." What the scholar discovers depends
on his "approach." The term implies a methodological perspectivism.

Dilthey tells the story of a nightmare that visited him sometime after he had begun to use the term *Weltanschauung.* As a
guest in a friend's house, he had been assigned a bed near a
reproduction of Raphael's *School of Athens,* and as he slept he
dreamt that the picture had come to life. All the famous thinkers
of antiquity began to rearrange themselves in groups according
to their *Weltanschauungen.* Slowly into the dream composition
came later thinkers: Kant, Schiller, Carlyle, Ranke, Guizot—
each of whom was drawn to one of the groups that had formed
around Plato or Heraclitus or Archimedes. Wandering back and
forth among the groups were other thinkers who tried to mediate
between them, but without success. In fact, the groups only
moved farther and farther apart, until they could communicate
only among themselves. The thinkers had become isolated in
their separate approaches to reality. Then Dilthey awoke from
his dream, which he interpreted as follows: No man can see any

reality steadily and see it whole. Each approach is partial and incommensurate with other approaches. "To contemplate all the aspects in their totality is denied to us."[8] But in his waking state there was for Dilthey a consolation: Each approach may be partial and confined, but each does disclose its own particular element of truth.

The history of literary criticism and scholarship yields its own version of Dilthey's nightmare. One need only paste different faces on Raphael's draped figures. On the far left, a group surrounds Freud, but refuses to converse with a nearby group surrounding Jung. Also on the left, of course, is another bearded German, Marx, with his numerous adherents; and still another German on the far right, Schleiermacher, is surrounded by a swarm of philologists, some of them with badges marked MLA. In the center, Plato and Aristotle cannot manage to hold their adherents together. Winters and Leavis move back and forth between them, following Coleridge, Arnold, and Johnson. Many other figures enter the composition. One group of them hesitates. They part, going towards different masters. They join again in puzzlement; they speak rapidly in French. At this point the restless dreamer wakes up.

What does the nightmare mean? Is Dilthey's mournful interpretation right? Does each critical approach present a partial truth forever trapped within its sponsoring perspective? Or worse, does each approach present a complete version of literature, as seen (and distorted) by its own perspective? To anyone desiring knowledge, either interpretation of the dream is a nightmare. Critical approaches cannot complement and support one another if they sponsor different meanings. We cannot look at a blackbird thirteen ways and thereby expect to come up with a truer blackbird—if our model assumes that each way of looking gives us a different blackbird. The net result would be thirteen blackbirds, and by analogy, thirteen interpretations of the same text. The perspectival implications of the word "approach" lead us logically to the skeptical conclusion that scholars and critics who use different approaches are just not perceiving or talking about the same reality.

Occasionally this impasse brings to somebody's mind the parable about the blind men and the elephant—the Anglo-Saxon version of Dilthey's nightmare. The blind man at the tail thinks the elephant is a snake, but the blind man at a leg thinks the elephant is a tree. But the parable itself is far more rational and comforting than the inference it is supposed to support in literary criticism. An intelligent and energetic blind man could conceivably move about and touch different parts of the creature and conclude that he was touching an elephant. But the word "approach" implies a different version of the story in which such a resolution would be impossible. In that story, several blind men are standing in different positions around one of the elephant's legs, yet they persist in their disagreement about what they are touching.

The story has to be told this way because no critic can approach textual meaning from any direction at all before there exists for him a meaning to be approached. Textual meaning is not like an elephant or a tree; it is not something out there to be approached from different points of view. It is not *there* for the critic in any sense until he has construed it. If a Marxist critic construes a text differently from a formalist critic, that is an irrelevant accident. No perspectival necessity requires him to do so. Marxist critics and formalist critics may be equally able to understand what a text means. What they usually differ in is the significance they give to that meaning.

Whatever a critic's approach may be, it must necessarily follow upon his understanding. An approach must be subsequent to a construing of what the written symbols mean. Nor is a construction of meaning something that is altered by different critical approaches. It is not a physical object that shows different configurations when viewed from different positions. Meaning is an object that exists *only* by virtue of a single, privileged, precritical approach. No matter how much critics may differ in critical approach, they must understand a text through the same precritical approach if they are to understand it at all. Why this must be so is the burden of the final part of this essay.

## IV. The Paradoxes of Perspectivism

I have argued that perspectivism, the theory that interpretation varies with the standpoint of the interpreter, is a root form of critical skepticism. Implicitly it rejects the possibility of an interpretation that is independent of the interpreter's own values and preconceptions; ultimately it repudiates correctness of interpretation as a possible goal. Since all interpretations are perspective-ridden, disparate interpretations can be equally correct, or what is the same thing, equally incorrect. But in that case what is left as an acceptable critical standard? Authenticity. A valid interpretation is one that represents an authentic realization of meaning through one's own perspective, or through that of one's time and culture. The practical aim of perspectivism can be expressed in positive terms as an attempt to replace the meaningless criterion of correctness with the presumably meaningful criterion of authenticity.

This explains why the issue was not entirely resolvable when conservative scholars attacked Roland Barthes's perspectivist interpretations of Racine; the terms of the debate were incommensurate. An "authentic" interpretation is not diminished in its authenticity just because it is "incorrect." This same irreconcilable clash of standards rendered inconclusive the similar polemics in biblical studies between "correct" interpreters like Karl Barth and "authentic" interpreters like Rudolph Bultmann. Obviously, debates about concrete interpretations cannot be settled before having resolved this fundamental conflict of criteria. For perspectivists, validity is entirely a function of the encounter between a text and one's inescapable cultural self.

But what, after all, is a perspective? The metaphor is spatial and visual, while the matter at hand is neither. If we were required momentarily to abandon the metaphor in favor of more descriptive terms, we would be forced to the realization that the visual metaphor refers to Kant's Copernican revolution in philosophy. Perspectivism is a version of the Kantian insight that

man's experience is preaccommodated to his categories of experience. The contribution to modern thought of Dilthey and others
was in extending the Kantian insight beyond the abstract, universal realms of science and mathematics into the richer, more
complex domains of cultural experience. Conscious of his debt
to Kant, Dilthey conceived his theoretical work on interpretation as part of a larger program which he called the "Critique of
Historical Reason."

What is popularly called a "perspective" refers to a theory
which in its classical and adequate form had nothing to do with
the visual metaphor. Hence, at this point, my exposition must
itself become less metaphorical and, philosophically, more serious. Kant postulated a universal structure in human subjectivity
which constitutes experience, and which thereby guarantees the
possibility of scientific knowledge. Dilthey and others postulated
that, beyond this universal subjectivity, there exists a cultural
subjectivity, structured by further categories which are analo-
gously constitutive of all cultural experience. Since Dilthey and
his fellow theorists were intimately aware that, under this conception, verbal meaning is entirely relative to cultural subjectivity, it may be instructive to ask more particularly how they
managed to eschew the skeptical conclusions of Dilthey's nightmare.

The problem is certainly a grave one. If all interpretation is
constituted by the interpreter's own cultural categories, how can
he possibly understand meanings that are constituted by different cultural categories? Dilthey's answer was straightforward
and perfectly within the sponsoring Kantian tradition. We can
understand culturally alien meanings because we are able to
adopt culturally alien categories. Admittedly, we can understand Racine only through those alien categories that are constitutive of his meaning—only through his perspective. Yet we *can*
adopt his categories; for cultural subjectivity is not an epistemological ultimate, comparable to Kant's universal system of categories. Cultural subjectivity is not innate, but acquired; it derives from a potential, present in every man, that is capable of
sponsoring an indefinite number of culturally conditioned cate-

gorial systems. It is within the capacity of every individual to imagine himself other than he is, to realize in himself another human or cultural possibility.

But the metaphor of perspective compels a different conclusion. Since every man sees the world from a different perspective, each one of us would have to misunderstand the other in his own way. That is the lesson taught by the analogy of visual perception. Misleading as it is, the analogy is with us and must be recognized as one of *our* cultural categories. Let me therefore introduce the first of my two paradoxes by taking the visual analogy seriously. I am led to the following skeptical argument:

1. Every object appears differently from different perspectives.
2. An interpreter always views a text in a perspective that is different from the author's.
3. Therefore, the meaning perceived by an interpreter must be at best subtly different from the meaning perceived by the author.

Yet even as a description of spatial-visual perception the argument is not empirically accurate. For instance, if I observe a building from one street and a friend looks at it from another street, the differences in what we see are indeed attributable to our different perspectives. Even if we were standing on the same street, just a few feet apart, differences would exist. The paradox is that, despite these differences, both of us perceive (i.e., visually interpret) the very same building. We see, that is, an object which is not entirely visible from *any* perspective, yet nevertheless we perceive it, know it, recognize it together; for by an imaginative extension we are always visually completing and correcting the partial view we get from a single perspective, just as binocular vision completes and corrects monocular perspective effects. If I see only one side of the building, I still know that it has other sides, and that the object of my perception is a whole building, not just the side that I see. My separated friend and I are therefore quite correct when we agree that we are seeing the same thing, and equally correct in assuming that the explicit components of our perception are nonetheless different. The

paradox involved here is that of the intentionality of consciousness—as explored in the work of Brentano, Meinong and Husserl. And it is a paradox which completely subverts the naiver
assumptions of popular perspectivism. Perspective-effects do
not necessarily distort and relativize what we understand. Anyone who takes the perspectivist metaphor seriously is forced by
the empirical facts of visual perception to reverse his original
inference, and conclude that a diversity of perspectives does
not necessarily compel a diversity of understood meanings.

The skeptical perspectivist does better, therefore, if he retreats
to the more adequate premises of the Kantian argument. This is
his most powerful line of defense, and from it he can argue quite
correctly that my building can be quite different from my
friend's even if we trade places and view it from an identical
physical perspective. My building is not a mere physical given
but an object constituted by my own special categorial system.
By the same token, every interpretation of verbal meaning is
constituted by the categories through which it is construed. Yet,
for everyone who looks at it, a building stands there as an object
of some sort. Verbal meaning is not an object like that. As a
construction from a mute text, meaning has existence only in
consciousness. Apart from the categories through which it is
construed, meaning can have no existence at all. This, then, is
the second and more important paradox of perspectivism. By an
extension of the great Kantian insight on which it is ultimately
based, interpretive perspectivism argues for the constitutive nature of cultural categories. In its deepest significance therefore,
perspectivism implies that verbal meaning exists *only* by virtue
of the perspective which gives it existence. And this compels the
conclusion that verbal meaning can exist only from one perspective. Again, under this second paradox, perspectivism once
more has to repudiate its naive skeptical conclusions. No longer
can it suppose that a meaning appears differently from different
perspectives, but is compelled to concede the absolute impossibility of viewing *meaning* from different perspectives.

It is an evasion at best to argue that the interpreter's alien
perspective distorts meaning, for it is impossible to distort some-

thing that cannot even exist by means of an alien perspective. The radical perspectivists are not radical enough by half. When, for instance, H. G. Gadamer speaks of a fusion of perspectives, a *Horizontverschmelzung*, he overlooks the paradox that this intermediate perspective can no longer possess the meaning it pretends to carry into the contemporary world. Of course, the words of a text can be respoken from a new perspective and a new meaning formulated. Of course, as some critics insist, the reader can become a self-imaging author. But a text cannot be *interpreted* from a perspective different from the original author's. Meaning is understood from the perspective that lends existence to meaning. Any other procedure is not interpretation but authorship.

Every act of interpretation involves, therefore, at least two perspectives, that of the author and that of the interpreter. The perspectives are entertained both at once, as in normal binocular vision. Far from being an extraordinary or illusory feat, this entertaining of two perspectives at once is the ground of all human intercourse, and a universal fact of speech which the linguists have called the "doubling of personality."[9] When we speak or interpret speech, we are never trapped in a single matrix of spiritual categories; we are never merely listeners or merely speakers; we are both at once. Readers of this essay—emphatically those who are disagreeing with my argument—are here and now practicing both interpretation and criticism, are entertaining two perspectives at once. For, my meaning exists and is construed only from my perspective, while the simultaneous criticism of that meaning implies a different perspective. The empirical actuality of this double perspective, universal in verbal intercourse, calls in doubt a basic premise of hermeneutical relativism and, with it, most of the presently fashionable forms of cognitive atheism.

# 4

# Stylistics and Synonymity

## I. Synonymity and the Basic Postulate of Stylistics

In this chapter I shall be less concerned with stylistics as a practical method than with its characteristic assumptions, which I attack without any intention to impugn the usefulness of stylistic analysis, currently a feature of much literary criticism. My main purpose is the positive one of defending the existence and importance of synonymity, that is, the expression of an absolutely identical meaning through different linguistic forms. In conducting this defense of synonymity, it happens to be logically necessary to attack the postulate that, given an identical context, a difference in linguistic form compels a difference in meaning— a postulate that I take to be a basic assumption of stylistics. Since that postulate is often true for specific cases, the practice of stylistics can be useful and valid. The object of my attack is simply the false methodological optimism that seeks in stylistic analysis a reliable system of interpretation. That methodological hope, being falsely based, can never be realized. Even in context, meaning cannot be reliably decided or deduced on the basis of linguistic form. That is the Gödel's theorem of language, a grasp of which might discourage excessive reliance on ever more refined methods of linguistic analysis.

The main point of this paper can be summed up as an argument for the variability of the relations between "form" and "content" in language, a variability that, by its nature, cannot be securely fixed by any combination of linguistic rules, conventions, and situational constraints. Since this argument concerns a general feature of language, it might seem arbitrary and provincial to center the discussion on stylistics, unless the reader

understands that the basic postulate of stylistics is here taken to
represent an assumption widely held in several related fields. For
instance, in anthropology and epistemology one finds a version
of the stylistics postulate in the Whorf-Sapir hypothesis, sometimes called "linguistic determinism."[1] Here again the issue is
not whether forms of the mother tongue sometimes constrain
forms of thought, but whether they always necessarily do so. In
this latter, strong form of the theory, not consistently held by
Whorf, linguistic determinism, like the stylistics postulate, is the
mortal enemy of synonymity.[2] But the reverse is also true.
Synonymity is the mortal enemy of linguistic determinism,
which holds that the form of language necessarily constitutes the
form of thought. That cannot be so if synonymity occurs, since
differences in form obviously do not in synonymous instances
compel differences in thought. A good deal hinges on whether
"The dog bit John" can carry exactly the same meaning as "John
was bitten by the dog."

Among philosophers as well as linguists the battle is still
joined between those who view the correlation between meaning
and linguistic form as strictly determined by convention, and
those who argue (as I shall) for the essential indeterminacy of the
relationship between meaning and form.[3] Plato's *Cratylus* aside,
the philosophical dialogue that forms the *locus classicus* of this
debate is the following:

> "You're holding it upside down!" Alice interrupted.
> "To be sure I was!" Humpty Dumpty said gaily, as she
> turned it round for him. "I thought it looked a little queer. As
> I was saying, that *seems* to be done right—though I haven't
> time to look it over thoroughly just now—and that shows that
> there are three hundred and sixty-four days when you might
> get un-birthday presents—"
> "Certainly," said Alice.
> "And only *one* for birthday presents, you know. There's
> glory for you!"
> "I don't know what you mean by 'glory,' " Alice said.
> Humpty Dumpty smiled contemptuously. "Of course you

don't—till I tell you. I meant 'there's a nice knock-down
argument for you!'"

"But 'glory' doesn't mean 'a nice knock-down argument',"
Alice objected.

"When *I* use a word," Humpty Dumpty said in rather a
scornful tone, "it means just what I choose it to mean—
neither more nor less."

"The question is," said Alice, "whether you *can* make words
mean different things."

"The question is," said Humpty Dumpty, "which is to be
master—that's all."

Alice was too much puzzled to say anything, so after a
minute Humpty Dumpty began again. "They've a temper,
some of them—particularly verbs, they're the proudest—
adjectives you can do anything with, but not verbs—however, *I* can manage the whole lot! Impenetrability! That's what
*I* say!"

"Would you tell me, please," said Alice, "what that means?"

"Now you talk like a reasonable child," said Humpty
Dumpty, looking very much pleased. "I meant by 'impenetrability' that we've had enough of that subject, and it would
be just as well if you'd mention what you mean to do next,
as I suppose you don't intend to stop here all the rest of your
life."

"That's a great deal to make one word mean," Alice said
in a thoughtful tone.

"When I make a word do a lot of work like that,"
said Humpty Dumpty, "I always pay it extra."[4]

In his learned and witty book, *The Philosopher's Alice*, Peter
Heath lists fifteen discussions of this passage—a partial list.[5]
Most of the discussions turn on Humpty Dumpty's stipulative
definition of the word "glory," which normally carries a meaning unlike his stipulated one. Now, stipulative definition may
indeed have been what Carroll had mainly in mind, but he might
also have been concerned with the troublesome problem of
implication, and hence with what philosophers, following J. L.
Austin, now call the "illocutionary force" of an utterance.[6] For
in actual speech, Humpty Dumpty would not necessarily have
been defying language conventions if in saying "There's glory for

you" he had meant "There's a glorious argument for you." His utterance would then simply have the illocutionary force of a boast about his cleverness in argument. But in that case, "There's glory" would have the force of "There's a gloriously clever argument." And since a gloriously clever argument is a nice knock-down argument, the latter is just what "glory" could indeed mean in Humpty Dumpty's conversation. Alice's well-known literal-mindedness (not to mention her ignorance of the writings of J. L. Austin) could then be seen as calling forth Humpty Dumpty's impatient irony in his subsequent remarks. Several native speakers of English have informed me that this interpretation is possible, thus proving that Humpty Dumpty has not exceeded the linguistic norms of English.

Theorists of style have shown some interest in Austin's theories of illocutionary force, and therefore might possibly accept my defense of Humpty Dumpty's linguistic propriety. But the theorist of style would undoubtedly balk were I to make this further claim: If Humpty Dumpty had said from the start, "There's a nice knock-down argument for you," his meaning would have been exactly the same as it was when he said, "There's glory for you." In a much more sophisticated and authoritative way, the theorist of style would undoubtedly make the same objection against my interpretation that Alice made against Humpty Dumpty's definition. For if Humpty Dumpty's theory is right, the basic postulate of stylistics must be wrong. Humpty Dumpty, a free spirit and true believer in synonymity,  is the enemy of the stylistics postulate, of strict conventionism, and all other forms of linguistic determinism, and is hence one of the heroes of this chapter.

## II. Synonymity and Analyticity

The bulkiest literature on the subject of synonymy is to be found neither in literary theory, linguistics, or speech-act theory, but in analytic philosophy. Since the late 1940s analytic philosophers have debated the possibility of synonymy in a number of vigorous articles, all written by philosophers of stature, such as

Quine, Goodman, Carnap, Grice, Strawson, Mates, Linsky, Pap, Ziff, and several others.[7] While I have found these discussions highly stimulating and helpful to my thinking, I have not found them directly relevant to my present subject. Nonetheless, because of the high quality of this work, some brief explanation is owed the reader as to why I shall not be referring to these philosophical debates.

In the first place, the concept of synonymity as defined in these writings is not the concept I am concerned with here. The criterion of synonymity that is generally used in these discussions is the criterion of universal substitutability. If *unmarried men* cannot always be substituted for *bachelors* without changing the meaning or the truth of the statement, then the two items are not synonymous. But this paper is focused on a different criterion: that of occasional substitutability. If the two items instanced above could ever be substituted without changing the meaning of the utterance, my more modest thesis about synonymity would be proved.

The second reason for the obliqueness of these debates to my present subject is their connection of synonymity with logical analyticity. An analytic judgment is one whose truth is systematically necessary quite apart from the judgment's connection with experience. Thus, in the system of arithmetic, the judgments $4=4$, $2+2=4$, $3+1=4$ are analytical, since all of them can be deduced from definitions by units: $2=1+1$, $3=1+1+1$, $4=1+1+1+1$. If substitutions are made on the basis of these unit definitions, all the first set of statements can be reduced to tautologies such as $4=4$. Thus, $2+2=4$ is reducible by substitution to $1+1+1+1=1+1+1+1$, a tautology, and thus, within the system, a necessary truth.[8] To those concerned with the nature of analytic judgments, substitutability obviously becomes a central issue, as does the cosubstitutability of words and phrases, which is to say, synonymity. Only through synonymy can the presumably analytic judgment "A is B" be reduced to the tautology "A is A."

The subject of analytic judgment is greatly interesting. It has weighty implications for epistemology and logic. It is, I think, almost totally irrelevant to occasional synonymity in natural languages, the subject of the present paper. In the natural languages, one almost never encounters synonymy of the form A is B. One is much more likely to encounter synonymy between sentences of different linguistic form. On this point, a logician who is also a stylist is worth quoting:

> We could not even have the appearance of judgment in *"A* is *A"* if we had not at least the difference of position in the different *A*'s; and we can not have the reality of judgment, unless some difference actually enters into the content of what we assert.
> We never at any time wish to use tautologies. No one is so foolish in ordinary life as to try to assert without some difference. We say indeed "I am myself," and "Man is man and master of his fate." But such sayings as these are no tautologies. They emphasize an attribute of the subject which some consideration or passing change may have threatened to obscure.... But mere tautology with deliberate purpose we never commit. Every judgment is essentially synthetical.[9]

I quote F. H. Bradley neither to praise or blame his stand on analytical judgments, but to applaud his accuracy in describing our normal use of language. His denial of synonymity in "Man is man" is surely accurate for most conceivable uses of that phrase, even though it is a point that has no necessary application to logical systems. But fortunately synonymy does not stand or fall on examples like "East is East and West is West," for which Bradley's observations hold, as they do also for the famous analytic judgment of Gertrude Stein: "A rose is a rose is a rose." For Bradley's reasons and others, each of those roses is different. But Bradley's reasoning would not necessarily deny synonymity to the following two sentences:

A rose is the flower of a dicot.
A rose is the flower of a dicotyledonous plant.

Nor, on Bradley's principles, would there be any grounds for denying synonymy in "A rose is *eine Rose*." Indeed, on his principle of communicative purposiveness there would be good reason for asserting synonymy in both cases.

### III. What is Style?

Normally by style we mean the linguistic form of an utterance considered apart from its meaning, and this is so whether or not we accept the postulate that style is always constitutive of meaning. Anyone who reads stylistic analyses, however, must be struck by the great variety of linguistic traits that are named stylistic traits: lexical choices, clause types, word order, phonemic patterns, rhythm, word length, etymology, sentence length, norm deviation, and others. This variety points to one of the difficulties in the very concept of linguistic form: the uncertainty whether a trait should be judged a form or a content.

Lexical substitutions, for instance, may be irrelevant to almost every other aspect of form: syntax, rhythm, sentence length, and so forth, so long as the words happen to have the same rhythmic stresses and belong to the same grammatical category. Such would be the case if Humpty Dumpty had said, "There's brilliance for you" instead of "There's glory for you." Unless the sounds per se of the two nouns were deemed significant, a stylistic discrimination of the two sentences would be confined to the semantic distinctions between *glory* and *brilliance*. But obviously the semantic differences of *glory* and *brilliance* do not directly correspond to their difference in phonemic form, but depend, rather, on their different "content." But then stylistic or formal analysis would already be content analysis. Hence, if we were inferring a difference in content from the difference in the form that constitutes content, we would have just begged the question, a point that would be obvious if in English *brilliance* and *glory* happened to have the same content.

At a still higher level of analysis, however, the semantic distinction between *glory* and *brilliance* could indeed constitute a formal or stylistic distinction. If the functional content of *glory* pertained to a quality of Humpty Dumpty's argument, while that of *brilliance* pertained to a quality of his mind, these two different contents could function as the vehicle for two different higher-level implications, say, disinterested admiration of the argument-as-an-argument versus self-praise. A linguistic phenomenon, it seems to me, can be called form or style when it is itself conceived as a vehicle for some further meaning. But that very same phenomenon can be called content when it is conceived as the representamen of a still lower-level phenomenon. Some literary theorists have held that form and content are invalid distinctions in language (a corollary to the postulate that style constitutes meaning), but another inference also offers itself: Form and content are essential distinctions that are entirely relative to a level of linguistic description.

A definition of style as a concept entirely relative to a particular level of analysis is supported by the continued use of the descriptive levels that have evolved in linguistics. The standard fields of linguistic science continue to imply a hierarchy of descriptive levels in language, that is, phonetics, phonology, morphology, grammar, and semantics.[10] This hierarchical system provides a well-tested model of language in which a lower-level phenomenon functions as the vehicle for a higher-level one. For instance, a large class of sounds, potentially an infinite number of slightly different ones, can function as the vehicle for a single phoneme; a class of a few different phonemes can function as the vehicle for a single morpheme. The morpheme *s*, for instance, used as a plural or possessive in English, is represented by at least two phonemes, *s* and *z*. The morpheme *d*, used to mark past tense, is represented phonemically by *d*, *t*, and *ed*. At the phonemic level, *dogs* and *cats* have different endings, but at the morphemic level they have absolutely identical endings. Their two different final phonemes are vehicles for the self-same morpheme. In other words, the style of the final sounds is different, but their meaning is the same. On the other hand, just the reverse asymmetry holds with *dogs* and *dog's*. The phonemic style of the endings is the same, but the morphemic meanings are different.

Of course, for my purposes, the more interesting asymmetry between style and meaning is the first case in which various different phonemes represent the same morpheme. Still more interesting is the fact of lower-level stylistic irrelevance. The final phonemes, for instance, of *mailed* and *missed* are indeed perceivable by all native speakers of English, but differences are not perceived as being semantically or linguistically operative.

Such variations in the functionality of stylistic differences is a subject to which I shall return, as the astute reader may guess.

Style, then, is a relative concept that depends on the level of analysis. What is style from the standpoint of a higher level is meaning from the standpoint of a lower one. Going back to the list of traits that are normally discussed in stylistic analyses, one sees that sound patterns, lexical choices, and the rest do not automatically qualify as stylistic features. A linguistic trait becomes a feature of style only with respect to a higher-level meaning for which it is the vehicle, but lower-level features are not always functional at a higher level.[11] Nothing in language is style or form per se, any more than it is meaning or content per se. Style is constitutive of meaning only when stylistic traits continue to be functional at the higher-level meanings they represent. In a given context, *spilled milk* might be semantically distinct from *spilt milk*, in which case the stylistic differences would be constitutive. Such participation of phonemic style in higher-level meaning is a frequent occurrence in poetry. But the opposite case is easily imagined. Stylistic differences need not always participate in or at all affect higher-level meanings.

If style, on the other hand, is *defined* as the system of linguistic traits which do participate in higher-level meanings, then the postulate that style is part of meaning becomes an empty tautology which simply states that style is part of meaning whenever it is part of meaning. One simply begs the question at issue to define style in advance as actualized meaning.

## IV. Why Perfect Synonymity is Widely Doubted

One reason stylistics appears to hold promise of a methodological *blaue Blume* for literary interpretation is the common knowledge, supported by literary instruction, that absolute synonymity is impossible. No doubt this doctrine really is true, by and large, for poetry. If a poetic phrase is changed, it will almost always be taken as having a changed meaning. But does the doctrine hold always for all of poetry? Or is it, rather, true about ninety percent of the time, or maybe eighty-five percent of the time? To answer that question with assurance, we could perform either of two tasks: we could show that poetry is by nature incapable of sustaining synonymy, or we could test all of poetry. But to do the first would be simply to deny the name of poetry to speech that sustained synonymy, even if others called the speech poetry, and thus to banish the question by stipulation rather than answer it. And to do the second, to test all of poetry, would be wasted effort. After all our labor, we would still be unable to speak with assurance about poems not yet composed. In the present and foreseeable state of our knowledge, we cannot reliably assert nonsynonymy for all poetry unless we can also assert nonsynonymy for all speech. The difference between a practical rule of thumb that is true eighty-five percent of the time and a genuine universal is not a mere fifteen percent. It is an unbridgeable abyss. A rule of thumb cannot be relied on in any particular instance. Unless synonymy is impossible in speech, we cannot be sure it is impossible in poetry.

But synonymy *is* impossible in speech. This larger assertion is widely stated or implied. Even technical prose is subject to stylistic analysis; even there absolute synonymy is impossible. Hence, the doctrine of nonsynonymy must hold *a fortiori* for poetry and the rest of imaginative literature. Nowhere in prose or verse can "The dog bit John" be synonymous with "John was bitten by the dog." Literary theory must extend this doctrine to all utterances, for only if the principle of nonsynonymy governs all of speech can the authority of stylistics be secure within the literary domain.

The universalistic doctrine of nonsynonymy seems so obvious that it need not even be stated, and usually is not. It is already believed by most persons, including many who are quite indifferent to poetry and literary theory. Obviously the doctrine must enjoy powerful support from our ordinary linguistic experience. If our native intuitions inform us that synonymy is impossible, the burden of proof is on anybody who claims that synonymy is not only possible, but widespread.

To make his task even more difficult, the defender of synonymy must also, apparently, dissent from the learned researches of historical lexicography. Philology informs us that words which may once have become very close in meaning tend thereafter to diverge from one another, or else one of them tends to drop out of use. If *pretty* meant exactly the same as *beautiful* why should speakers continue to use *beautiful*, a word that takes more time and effort to say? Henry Bradley and Otto Jesperson, among others, have shown this functionalism to be powerfully at work in language evolution. A kind of Darwinian functionalism fosters semantic differentiations, and has been in English a source of great lexical richness (*pig* vs. *pork*, *sheep* vs. *mutton* etc.). No doubt all languages show the same lexical tendency either toward differentiation or disappearance. If so, historical lexicology adds its authority to our native intuitions about words, and to literary theory, against the possibility of perfect synonymity.

But the reason for such unanimity lies entirely in the way the question about synonymy is normally posed. If the man in the street is asked whether *pretty* means the same as *beautiful*, he is entirely right to answer "No," when the question is so framed. And even if the words are contextualized in sentences, the experiment yields the same results. "She's a pretty girl" and "She's a beautiful girl" carry different meanings for the native speaker—when the sentences are presented in isolation. But this usual way of testing for synonymy is in some respects an entirely artificial experiment. Perhaps a kind of test could be conducted with pairs like *pretty* and *beautiful* which avoided such abnormal decontextualizing. If so, it would be a more informative and significant experiment, for it would take into account another native intuition about language, namely the enormous flexibility and variability of language in actual use. One kind of intuition tells us that *pretty* and *beautiful* in isolation carry different meanings. Can tests of synonymity be devised for our second kind of intuition about the flexibility of language in actual use?

To find out, I devised a test with some words that have been a leitmotif in philosophical discussions of synonymity: *bachelors* and *unmarried men*. Presented in isolation, these expressions are indeed semantically distinct. *Bachelors* sounds informal; *unmarried men* sounds impersonal and legalistic. Psycholinguistic tests, moreover, have proved that single words usually carry different meanings than do their phrasal near-equivalents—when the two are paired off in isolation.[12] As between the sentences "This is a club for bachelors" and "This is a club for unmarried men," one feels a tonal difference that amounts to a difference in meaning. But, instead of presenting these sentences in isolation, suppose we invent an actual use for them—as in a club charter:

This is a club for bachelors. Experience having shown that this town offers no convenient facility where unmarried men can eat, drink, and converse in peace with fellow bachelors, nor any place where they can resort free from the gaze of unmarried women, we, the undersigned do hereby charter and found the Bower Club where only unmarried men, that is, bachelors, may enter its precincts as members or as guests.

This document thrice uses "bachelors," twice "unmarried men," and once the pronoun "they." By the simple device of substituting the word *bachelors* for the corresponding phrase, and vice versa, you can perform an experiment which is different from the one that presents these words in isolation. You show the two documents thus created to a number of literate native speakers, and you will discover, as I have, that, without exception, they will tell you it is a matter of total indifference which document the club should use; that the two charters mean exactly the same thing; that they are in fact perfectly synonymous. Moreover, when we consider that the documents are not linguistically eccentric, and either could, in fact, be a club charter, we conclude that our experiment is more, not less, informative about language in use than is an experiment with isolated words or sentences.

To resolve the apparently contradictory results of these two sorts of experiment, what language model or other means of explanation can be found? No one familiar with English would be likely to claim that *bachelors* and *unmarried men* presented in isolation are perfectly synonymous. Yet no native speaker except a theorist or professor of literature would be likely to deny their perfect synonymity in the particular usage just described. I would suggest the following explanation for our apparently conflicting linguistic intuitions. When presented in isolation, the word *bachelor* and the phrase *unmarried men* each embraces a different range of potential meanings in use, a different range of semantic possibilities. On the other hand, we know that not every meaning potential is actualized in every use of a word. Furthermore, and this is the more relevant point in explaining the contrary intuitions, the different isolated expressions possess different ranges of *probable* meanings in use. The decisive semantic distinctions of words presented in isolation are their different meaning-probabilities. *Unmarried men* has a high probability of use in legal or sociological contexts; *bachelors* has a high probability of use in less technical contexts. *We intuit these different semantic probabilities from our past linguistic experience, and when we encounter the words in isolation, we posit their most usual past meaning as their normal meaning-in-isolation. On the other hand, when we encounter these words in actual use, their semantic probabilities, and accordingly, our meaning expectations, may shift rather far from this norm.*

I won't argue at length for this hypothesis, particularly as it is less a matter for abstract argument than for empirical testing. The tests that I know of, conducted by Brown, Deese, and other psycholinguists, entirely support the explanation just sketched out. [13] Their research indicates that we begin to interpret linguistic meanings by positing probable meanings based on past usage; then we proceed to qualify and amend this conjecture by further experience of the ongoing utterance. But when we encounter a word in isolation we remain stuck in our original semantic postulate, which is always taken from a very restricted number of semantic and grammatical categories, all of relatively high frequency for that word. (The same principle holds, mutatis mutandis, for sentences presented in isolation.) Hence, when the man in the street says that different words have different meanings, he refers to his original meaning postulates for them, as based on his experience of their most frequent meanings in past use. In attending to speech we must always begin with such postulates, since if we lacked *any* firm meaning-expectations we could not begin to understand any utterance. We need confidence that not all our meaning postulates are in doubt all the time. That is why the man in the street is right in finding different nuances in different isolated words.

On the other hand, if we did not, in actual speech, constantly adjust our original meaning postulates, we could never speak or understand language with novelty, flexibility or precision. Language requires not only our intuition of a firm isolated meaning, but also our counter intuition that this meaning is only provisional. Both intuitions are right; they do not conflict; they are, in fact, coordinate. Still, it is fair to say that the more comprehensive intuition is the one that goes beyond our isolated meaning-expectations and recognizes their provisional character whenever we actually use and understand language. The most striking evidence of this is rarely, if ever, analyzed by proponents of nonsynonymity. It is simply this: the relation of form to meaning is so very flexible, even to the point of indeterminacy, that a word, or even a whole written text, is not necessarily synonymous with itself. The potential nonsynonymy of texts with themselves is, in fact, the chief raison d'être of literary scholarship. But if language is sufficiently flexible to allow the same words different meanings, it is sufficiently flexible to allow different words the same meaning. On the model of speech just presented, the meaning-potentials of texts using different words can overlap in an area of total synonymity, and this potential for synonymity can be actualized in speech.

## V. Synonymity and Linguistics

I have already illustrated some of the highly variable relations between manner and meaning in language by presenting examples of morpheme synonymy (*s, z* and *d, t, ed*). I want to focus now on some further examples of variability at lower and at higher linguistic levels, to indicate that this was by no means a special case, and also to call attention to some recent work in linguistics that strongly buttresses the case for synonymity.

The most elementary place to start is at the physical level of speech, where different physical sounds can represent one and the same speech sound. Indeed, the discovery of this primal example of synonymity—the phoneme—marked the beginning of modern linguistic science. Within limits, differences in our physical style of speech (and each of us makes slightly different noises, as the voice spectrograph shows), do not constitute differences in meaning at the level of the phoneme. And yet the example is not as clear-cut as it might first appear. Every speaker of grapholectic, or so-called standard English, uses, it is true, the same set of phonemes. But the synonymy of these phonemes despite the different styles of their presentation is not an absolute universal. Phoneme synonymy is, rather, a variable that depends upon the occasion. In standard English a midwesterner and a southerner use identical phonemes—unless and until a regional style of speech becomes itself functional in meaning. We know that this does happen—for instance, when regional accents are rendered in fictional dialogue. On the other hand, we know that it does not normally happen in technical discourse. The meanings in this essay would not be altered one scintilla if the paper were being read aloud in his regional accent by a southerner, a midwesterner, a Scotsman, or an Australian. Between the two extremes of fictional dialogue and technical discourse, one can imagine many intermediate degrees of semantic functionality in the physical, phonetic style of presentation, depending on the particular utterance.

The very same variability in the connection between manner and meaning occurs at the level of the word. Setting aside phonetics and the question of regional accents, we can say that two words that are different *phonemically* may nevertheless be identical lexically. Here obvious examples are *tomāto* and *tomahto, eether* and *either,* and so on. In some cases these phonemically different words coexist in the same regional accent, even in the speech of a single individual. On the other hand, it sometimes undoubtedly happens that a phonemic choice between, say *eether* and *either* can indeed be functional in higher-level meaning, particularly in cases where social class, like regional accent, is deliberately made part of the meaning to be conveyed.

Going one step higher in the linguistic hierarchy, stylistic choices at the lexical level exhibit the same semantic variability. The word *jacket* may not be synonymous with the word *coat* in a particular use, but on another occasion it might be completely synonymous. A still better example is the pair of words *synonymity* and *synonymy*. Some readers may have noticed that I have used these two words randomly in this paper, but without any distinction of meaning of any kind. But when I was devising a title for the paper, my choice between the two words was not random at all. I decided that the word *synonymity* in the title would convey my meaning more clearly because of its more obvious association with the familiar word *synonym*. That is the sort of semantic distinction that arises when a word is presented in isolation, or in the quasi-isolation of a title. In the title there would have been, in the minds of some readers, a semantic distinction between the two words. In the body of this paper there is none. At the lexical level, then, we find the same variability as we found on lower levels in the semantic functionality of stylistic choice.

The theoretical implications of the phenomena just described have been carefully drawn in a number of important articles and monographs by C. E. Bazell. The flavor of his argument can be inferred from the title of one of his essays, "The Correspondence Fallacy in Structural Linguistics." Although this piece and the others are complex, detailed, and technical, I believe their main point can be simply stated as follows without too much distortion: The correspondence fallacy in linguistics is the assumption that a structural or functional correspondence exists between lower and higher-level phenomena in language. Here, for instance, is a passage from the preface to Bazell's book *Linguistic Form*:

If it is possible to discover any aim common to all linguistic
schools, this aim is the reduction by terminological devices, of
the fundamental asymmetry of linguistic systems. If there are
phonemes, allophones and phonemic components, then there
must also be morphemes, allomorphs, and morphemic components. If there is a form and a substance of the expression,
then there must also be a form and a substance of the content. . . . There is hence perhaps room for a work which seeks
to stress the fundamental asymmetry of linguistic systems,
rather than to reduce it.[14]

In a later article, "The Sememe," Bazell explicitly stresses
one of the central points of this paper, namely "the total asymmetry of morphemic and sememic levels":

Glossematics presupposes a parallelism between the planes of
content and expression (no doubt an erroneous parallel), but
fails to pursue this parallelism with any consistency. . . . In
order that a unit of expression may be regarded from the
standpoint of content it is necessary that it should be isomor-
phous with a content. Which it may or may not be.[15]

Finally, from this same article, I quote a brief passage that
indicates one of the main reasons for the variability and asymmetry between linguistic levels:

It must not be supposed that an utterance can be split up into
sememes in the unique manner often possible for morphemes.
Just as morphemic analysis is liable to be less determinate than
phonemic analysis, so is sememic analysis liable to be more
indeterminate than morphemic analysis.[16]

Here Bazell has stated in another form what I have called the
Gödel's theorem of language—the intrinsic undecidability of the
correlations between linguistic levels. As higher-level phenomena are reached, correlations between levels become increasingly
indeterminate because the relations between the levels are
increasingly liable to asymmetries and variabilities that are not
strictly rule-governed. There could be no rule based on linguistic
form that could determine, for instance, whether or not a
meaning is ironic in whole or in part. That is not to say that an

ironic meaning is itself indeterminate, or that it couldn't be determined with as much certainty as any other meaning, but only that it, along with all other higher-level meanings, cannot be reliably decided on the basis of linguistic form.[17]

If Bazell's views, shared by many linguists, are correct, as I believe, it follows that stylistics is in principle unreliable for deciding meaning. We cannot, in fact, decide whether a trait of style is part of meaning until we know what the meaning is. Our knowledge of meaning determines the semantic functionality of style, not vice versa. From Bazell's analyses, it also follows that synonymy is in principle a linguistic possibility. Some linguists have always assumed that possibility, and indeed it is a moot question whether transformational theory could logically exist except on the assumption of synonymity.[18] Very recently, the linguistic possibility of synonymy has been ably defended by Roy Harris, a student of Bazell's, in a closely reasoned and carefully argued book called *Synonymy and Linguistic Analysis*.[19] In Harris's book may also be found a useful bibliography of books and articles pertaining to synonymity.

## VI. Synonymity and Speech-Act Theory

When J. L. Austin introduced the concept of illocutionary force into language analysis, he focused philosophical attention on a domain of discourse that had been attended to mainly by literary critics. Without necessarily accepting Austin's categories of description, one can applaud his current influence on the philosophical study of verbal communication. Before the advent of Austin, literary critics had, of course, recognized that a text might be categorized under different genres, and be interpreted differently according to the different conventions of the subsuming genres. Austin made a similar point about the whole realm of speech. In his terms, a word-sequence like "pass the salt" could have the illocutionary force of, say, a request or a command. In other words, the utterance could belong to either of those two different genres.

Literary critics when discussing genre have tended to fall into two camps, which for simplicity can be called the Aristotelean and the Crocean. Aristoteleans have held that genres are limited in number (whether by convention or the nature of things or a combination of both). Croceans have held that genres are fictitious entities that arbitrarily break up the infinite continuum of expressions, each expression being potentially sui generis. This literary debate has now reappeared in speech-act theory. Is the meaning of a speech act determined ultimately by a limited number of public conventions, or ultimately by the potentially limitless nuances of speakers' intentions? Are the genres of utterance strictly limited, or are they, rather, potentially limitless? No party to the debate doubts, of course, that speech acts are, in most of their aspects, conventional acts. The crucial question now debated by philosophers is whether they are and must be entirely convention-governed. Since this debate is a refined version of the argument between Alice and Humpty Dumpty, it is important for synonymity.

In the 1940s and early 50s, the two sides of the question were represented by Austin and Wittgenstein. Austin came down on the side of a quite limited number of conventional genres, and before his early death was still testing out those genres which had individual names in the English vocabulary, such as *order, command, request, entreaty,* and so on.[20] In this (provisional) limitation he was implicitly opposed by Wittgenstein:

> But how many kinds of sentence are there? Say assertion, question, and command?—There are *countless* kinds: countless different kinds of use of what we call 'signs,' 'words,' 'sentences.' And this multiplicity is not something fixed, given once for all; but new types of language, new language-games, as we may say, come into existence, and others become obsolete and get forgotten.[21]

More recently the debate has been continued by Max Black and John Searle on one side, with H. P. Grice and P. F. Strawson on the other.[22] The key terms have become "convention" and "intention," familiar terms of literary theory. Max Black, representing the conventionalist view, sums up his argument succinctly in the epigraph to his polemic against Grice:

> If you think that saying is different from the twitter of
> fledglings, can you prove a distinction, or is there no
> distinction?
>
> —Chuang-Tzu[23]

The implication is, unless convention is understood entirely to govern the meaning of speech, there is no adequate way to determine the meaning of speech. If the language-games are partly intention-governed, and hence "countless," there is no distinguishing between speech acts and the twitter of fledglings.

P. F. Strawson, implicitly defending Grice in his Oxford inaugural of November 1969, has had, I think, the last word in this debate. Both sides, he points out, agree that verbal meanings are largely determined by semantic and syntactic rules or conventions. Where they differ is on the character, origin, and omnipotence of those conventions. Strawson, toward the beginning of his lecture, tells an analytic-genetic "story" that is worth quoting at length:

> Suppose an utterer achieves a pre-conventional communica-
> tion success with a given audience by means of an utterance,
> say *x*. He has a complex intention *vis-à-vis* the audience of
> the sort which counts as a communication-intention and suc-
> ceeds in fulfilling that intention by uttering *x*. Let us suppose
> that the primary intention was such that the utterer *meant*
> that *p* by uttering *x*; and since by hypothesis, he achieved
> a communication-success, he was so *understood* by his audi-
> ence. Now if the same communication-problem presents itself
> later to the same utterer in relation to the same audience, the
> fact, known to both of them, that the utterer meant that
> *p* by uttering *x* before, gives the utterer a reason for uttering
> *x* again and the audience a reason for interpreting the utter-
> ance in the same way as before.(The reason each has is the
> knowledge that the other has the knowledge which he has.)

So it is easy to see how the utterance of $x$ could become established as between this utterer and this audience as a means of establishing that $p$. Because it has worked, it becomes established; and then it works *because* it is established. And it is easy to see how this story could be told so as to involve not just a group of two, but a wider group. So we can have a movement from an utterer pre-conventionally meaning that $p$ by an utterance of $x$ to the utterance-type $x$ conventionally meaning that $p$ within a group and thence back to utterer-members of the group meaning that $p$ by a token of the type, but now *in accordance with the conventions*....

There is no reason in principle why a pre-conventional utterance should not have a certain complexity—a kind of complexity which allowed an utterer, having achieved one communication-success, to achieve another by repeating one part of the utterance while varying the other part, what he means on the second occasion having something in common with, and something that differentiates it from, what he meant on the first occasion. And if he does thus achieve a second success, the way is open for a rudimentary *system* of utterance-types to become established, i.e. to become conventional within a group.

A system of conventions can be modified to meet needs which we can scarcely imagine existing before the system existed. And its modification and enrichment may in turn create the possibility of thoughts such as we cannot understand what it would be for one to have, without supposing such modification and enrichment to have taken place. In this way we can picture a kind of alternating development. Primitive communication-intentions and successes give rise to the emergence of a limited conventional meaning-system, which makes possible its own enrichment and development which in turn makes possible the enlargement of thought and of communication-needs to a point at which there is once more pressure on the existing resources of language which is in turn responsive to such pressure.[24]

Now, a conventionalist cannot tell a "story" like that. Only an intentionalist can. Until a conventionalist can explain how conventions could *arise*, and how they could *change*, as Strawson does, he has a very deficient, and, as it seems to me, very implausible theory of verbal meaning.

He suffers an additional embarrassment. The element of indeterminacy which intention apparently introduces, and which the conventionalist, with the stylistician, wishes to banish along with the twitter of birds, comes in by the back door, even under conventionalist theory. For any act of saying, "Pass the salt," there is always a degree of uncertainty about which convention is in effect. Is it an order, a command, a request, an entreaty, a supplication, and so on? If such uncertainty exists, then the word "convention" (which is often just an inexact label for semantic probabilities) becomes a mask that hides an infinite regress. For, which convention shall determine the applicable convention? And which convention shall determine that? If an auditor wants ever to get to the next sentence, he has to guess which *intention* governs the choice of convention. This inherent indeterminacy of genre-convention parallels the inherent indeterminacy of the correlation between linguistic meaning and linguistic form. Both are governed in part by intention, and thus provide parallel arguments for synonymity. To date (and I think permanently) the truth seems to lie with Grice, Strawson, and Humpty Dumpty rather than with Black and Searle and Alice.

## VII. Synonymity and Knowledge

The case is ready for summing up. Speech-act theory, in the form developed by Grice and Strawson reasserts the linguistic priority of intention and hence of mind. It asserts the indeterminacy, and hence the partial independence of meaning with respect to form and to convention. It follows that a guess about intention is in principle a permanent feature of interpretation which no methodological system could ever remove. The guess itself cannot be fully determined by stylistic features, nor can stylistic features definitively confirm the guess concerning intended meaning. (The guess partly constitutes stylistic features in any case.) The methodological hopes of stylistics are battered from the philosophical as well as the linguistic side.

On the other hand, stylistic analysis is not seriously injured by the attack, so long as it modifies its practical claims and relinquishes its confidence in its own methodological future. Stylistics cannot be a reliable method of determining meaning, nor a reliable method of confirming an interpretation, but neither can any other method perform those feats. Consequently, as a practical matter, stylistic analysis remains useful in the highest degree to the disciplines of interpretation. For stylistics may indeed provide clues that help induce interpretive guesses, and may indeed provide evidence that helps shift the weight of probability from one interpretation to another. Of course, in that sense, all interpretive arguments employ some of the tools of stylistics, whether or not they call themselves stylistics.

I observed at the beginning of this paper that synonymity must be the mortal enemy of systematic stylistics, since every case of synonymity instances differences of style that are entirely irrelevant to meaning. But it must now be added that synonymity is the bosom friend and close ally of systematic stylistics with respect to the goal it has set itself: genuine (objective) knowledge about meaning. Genuine knowledge in any field, that is, sharable and usable knowledge, depends upon the communication of propositions about reality. The final point of this essay is that you cannot have propositions (and hence shared knowledge) without also having synonymity.

It is an essential condition for conveying and using propositions about reality (including propositions about verbal meaning) that they be reexpressible in different contexts without altering the meaning of the proposition. (To alter the meaning of a proposition is to alter the proposition, which *is* a meaning.) It might be argued that what I am calling a proposition is simply a narrowly limited aspect of an expression's meaning. But that objection cannot pass muster. The knowledge that is actually shared and used in the humanities and the sciences is by no means limited to narrow and abstract propositions. Nor can we know what needs to be "abstracted" from an expression until we have already understood its proposition. There is no evident reason why the entire meaning of an expression could not be a proposition.

Suppose a proposition is stated by the expression "The earth goes around the sun." Now, is the following a different proposition? "The sun is circuited by the earth." The correct answer, I believe, is that the proposition might be the same or it might be different, depending, for instance, on whether the subject of the proposition was the sun in both cases. The fact that both statements refer to the same state of affairs does not make them the same proposition about that state of affairs.[25] But the sentences *could* express the same proposition because they *could* carry the same meaning.

Unless different sentences could carry the same meaning, we would always need to use the same sentence to convey the same proposition. But if we used the same sentence in a different context, it might, as every stylist knows, carry a different meaning, which is to say a different proposition. Hence in his excellent encyclopedia article on propositions, Alonzo Church speaks of the need for a notion

> independent alike of any particular expression in words and of any particular psychological act of judgment or conception—not the particular declarative sentence but the content or meaning which is common to the sentence and its translation into another language—not the particular judgment, but the objective content of the judgment which is capable of being the common property of many.[26]

Shared knowledge requires shared and reexpressible propositions. But if different linguistic forms must express different meanings, they must always express different propositions. The only linguistic definition of a proposition so far proposed that is free from this embarrassment is the following: "A proposition is the meaning of a class of synonymous sentences."[27]

# 5

# Three Dimensions of Hermeneutics

How important are the theoretical disagreements that now divide serious students of interpretation? How true is the resigned opinion that our various schools and approaches are like a multitude of warring sects, each with its own uncompromising theology? Is it the destiny of those who practice interpretation never to achieve an ecumenical harmony of theoretical principles? If that is our destiny, so much the worse for theory, which is then only the ideology of a sect, and so much the better for the common sense of a practitioner who disdains theory to get on with his work.

> For modes of faith let graceless zealots fight;
> His can't be wrong, whose life is in the right.

A theorist would be right to reply that the repudiation of theory in favor of common sense implies a theoretical position, and that the commonalty of common sense would seem to require a wide measure of theoretical agreement about the nature of a "sensible" or "good" interpretation. In my opinion, such implicit agreement is not only possible but already widely extant. The appearance of disagreement, which itself produces so many quarrels, can be traced back to a tendency of interpretive theory to lump together both what interpreters agree on and what in the nature of the case they can never agree on. The distinction in my title between various dimensions of hermeneutics suggests my ecumenical purpose; by separating the separable it may be possible to disclose areas of agreement shared by apparently conflicting theories.

74

As a first step, I propose that interpretive theories should not lump together the descriptive and the normative aspects of interpretation; that theorists should disengage the descriptive dimension of hermeneutics, which concerns the nature of interpretation, from the normative dimension, which concerns its goals. For the goals of interpretation are determined ultimately by value-preferences, and interpreters do not exhibit more agreement in their values than the generality of people. I know it is usual to argue, as Coleridge did, that certain values and therefore certain interpretive norms are permanently rooted in the nature of literature, that the normative is derived from the descriptive. I know why Coleridge and others have held this view in the history of literary theory; they have desired a permanent and universal sanction for certain evaluative norms for literature, and what more permanent sanction could exist than "the nature of literature"? By the same reasoning, it is convenient to derive permanent, normative principles of interpretation from "the nature of interpretation."

I find the structure of such reasoning entirely circular: good literature is that which conforms to the true nature of literature; good interpretation is that which conforms to the true nature of interpretation. But what is this "true nature" except a tautological rephrasing of "good literature" or "good interpretation"? Are there not numerous examples of bad literature or bad interpretation which do not conform to this true nature? Yet if these bad examples are pieces of literature, if they are instances of interpretation, they must exhibit the true nature of literature or of interpretation. The Coleridgean argument imports the normative into the descriptive from the beginning, by sleight of hand.

Stated bluntly, the nature of interpretation is to construe from a sign-system (for short, "text") something more than its physical presence. That is, the nature of a text is to mean whatever we construe it to mean. I am aware that theory should try to provide normative criteria for discriminating good from bad, legitimate from illegitimate constructions of a text, but mere theory cannot change the nature of interpretation. Indeed, we need a norm precisely because the nature of a text is to have no meaning except that which an interpreter wills into existence. We, not our texts, are the makers of the meanings we understand, a text being only an occasion for meaning, in itself an ambiguous form devoid of the consciousness where meaning abides. One meaning of a text can have no higher claim than another on the grounds that it derives from the "nature of interpretation," for all interpreted meanings are ontologically equal; they are all equally real. When we discriminate between legitimate and illegitimate meanings in "Lycidas," for example, we cannot claim merely to be describing the nature of Milton's text, for the text compliantly changes its nature from one interpreter to another. This ontological equality of all interpreted meanings shows forth in the fact that hermeneutic theory has sanctioned just about every conceivable norm of legitimacy in interpretation. From this historical fact I infer that interpretive norms are not really derived from theory, and that theory codifies *ex post facto* the interpretive norms we already prefer.

To take a central example from the history of interpretation: by the eighteenth century an impressive victory had been won over certain medieval modes of interpretation, so that by then anachronistic allegorizing seemed to be permanently repudiated. Under the post-medieval view, since Homer and Vergil were not Christian their texts could not legitimately be regarded as Christian allegories. Schleiermacher, in the late eighteenth century, was merely codifying the work of his humanistic predecessors when he stated the following as a universal canon of interpretation: "Everything in a given text which requires fuller interpretation must be explained and determined exclusively from the linguistic domain common to the author and his original public."[1] Under this principle, Christian allegorizing of the ancients is deprived of all legitimacy, and the way is thereby opened to an interpretation that is truly historical and scientific.

Or so it seemed to Schleiermacher. But the humanistic repudiation of anachronisms cannot be upheld on purely cognitive or logical grounds. Under Schleiermacher's canon, no text can legitimately mean at a later time what it could not have meant originally, but logic alone hardly supports this inference. The

medieval interpreters were well aware that Homer and Vergil had
been pagans who could not consciously have intended or communicated Christian meanings. The exegetes of the Middle Ages
implicitly held to another principle which can be stated as follows: "Everything in a given text which requires fuller interpretation need *not* be explained and determined exclusively from the
linguistic domain common to the author and his original public."
Which principle is logically the more compelling, this implicit
medieval one, or that of Schleiermacher? The answer is easy. The
medieval principle is logically stronger because self-evidently a
text can mean anything it has been understood to mean. If an
ancient text has been interpreted as a Christian allegory, that is
unanswerable proof that it can be so interpreted. Thus, the
illegitimacy of anachronistic allegory, implied by Schleiermacher's canon, is deduced neither from empirical fact nor
logic. His norm of legitimacy is not, of course, deduced at all; it is
chosen. It is based upon a value-preference, and not on theoretical
necessity. His preference for original meaning over anachronistic
meaning is ultimately an ethical choice. I would confidently
generalize from this example to assert that the normative dimension of interpretation is always in the last analysis an ethical
dimension.

At this point I shall not digress to take sides in the ethical
dispute between the anachronists and the historicists, for I wish to
deal with that issue at the end of this essay. But I do pause to
observe that the exegetical morality of the medieval allegorizers is
not necessarily less admirable than their logic. Indeed, it seems to
me that both Schleiermacher and those medieval interpreters
repudiated by his canon are following according to their different
lights the very same ethical principle. For anachronistic meaning
and original meaning have this in common: they are both attempts to achieve legitimacy under the criterion of the "best
meaning." In the history of interpretation it would seem to be a
constant principle that the "best meaning" is to be considered the
most legitimate meaning of a text. The differences arise in
defining "best." An interpreter of the thirteenth century could
argue that Christian allegory is a better meaning than the original,

*There is another possible move than ideology — which is what H. is claiming.*

pagan one, while a humanist of the Renaissance could respond that the original meaning in Antiquity is superior to any that could be imposed by the graceless culture of the Middle Ages. In the late eighteenth and early nineteenth century romantics like Schleiermacher could extend the humanist tradition with the argument that the original meaning is always the best meaning no matter what the provenance of the text, because every culture has infinite value in its own right; each culture is a note in the divine symphony, as Herder rhapsodized; or as Ranke preached, every age is immediate to God. Although we no longer shore up our historicism with such quasi-religious conceptions, the romantic ideal of cultural pluralism has continued to be the dominant ethical norm for interpretation during most of the nineteenth and twentieth centuries: it is more comprehensive and more humanizing to embrace the plurality of cultures than to be imprisoned in our own. We ought therefore to respect original meaning as the best meaning, the most legitimate norm for interpretation. Only recently has historicism turned back upon itself to announce that we *are* imprisoned in our own culture willy-nilly, and we must therefore return to a quasi-medieval conception of interpretation, namely that the best meaning (for that matter any meaning) must be anachronistic whether we like it or not. Under this recent conception, the "best meaning" reveals itself as a self-conscious, ethical choice as to what is best "for us today" according to some standard that is compelling in our present historical circumstances.

If the normative dimension of hermeneutics belongs, as I have argued, to the domain of ethical choice, is it nevertheless possible to discover truly universal principles of the sort Schleiermacher envisioned, principles that do not depend on the value-preferences of individual interpreters? Is there in hermeneutics an analytical dimension which, in contrast to the normative, is logically deductive, empirically descriptive, and neutral with respect to values and ethical choices? The spirit of the present age inclines us skeptically to assume that such a pretense of objective neutrality would merely be a mask for a particular set of values. Yet if we could manage to find an area of agreement shared by widely different interpretive sects, then the reality of a truly descriptive dimension of hermeneutics would come to seem more plausible. And if the area of theoretical agreement could be gradually enlarged, there might emerge a sense of community in the discipline of interpretation, a sense of belonging to a common enterprise.

## II

One example of a purely descriptive theoretical conception, and one that seems to me potentially fruitful, is the distinction between meaning and significance. When I first proposed this distinction my motivation was far from netural; I equated meaning simply with original meaning, and I wished to point up the integrity and permanence of original meaning.[2] This earlier discussion I now regard as being only a special application of a conception that is in principle universal. For the distinction between meaning and significance (and the clarifications it provides) are not limited to instances where meaning is equated with the author's original meaning; it holds as well for any and all instances of "anachronistic meaning."[3]

This universality in the distinction is readily seen if meaning is defined *tout court* as that which a text is taken to represent. No normative limitations are imported into the definition, since under it, meaning is simply meaning-for-an-interpreter. Moreover, the definition does not (and did not in my earlier discussion) limit itself merely to a paraphrasable or translatable "message," but embraces every aspect of representation, including the typographical and phonemic, which an interpreter construes. My earlier definition of meaning was too narrow and normative only in that it restricted meaning to those constructions where the interpreter is governed by his conception of the author's will. The enlarged definition now comprises constructions where authorial will is partly or totally disregarded.

The important feature of meaning as distinct from significance is that meaning is the determinate representation of a text for an interpreter. An interpreted text is always taken to represent

something, but that something can always be related to something else. Significance is meaning-as-related-to-something-else.
If an interpreter did not conceive a text's meaning to be *there* as an
occasion for contemplation or application, he would have nothing to think or talk about. Its thereness, its self-identity from
one moment to the next allows it to be contemplated. Thus, while
meaning is a principle of stability in an interpretation, significance embraces a principle of change. Meaning-for-an-interpreter
can stay the same although the meaningfulness (significance) of
that meaning can change with the changing contexts in which that
meaning is applied. An interpreter could, for instance, find the
following to be variously meaningful: "The cat is on the mat,"
depending on whether the cat has left the mat, on whether he likes
cats, and so on. The point is not that an interpreter must apply
meaning to changing contexts, but that he could do so and still be
able in every case to construe his text as representing an identical
meaning.

The main objection to this distinction between a principle of
stability and a principle of change has been that it fails to describe
what actually takes place in the process of interpretation. It is said
that the distinction proposes what is in fact a psychological
impossibility. If this were so, the objection would be fatal, since
empirical truth is the ultimate arbiter of theories in the practical
disciplines. But I doubt the empirical validity of the objection,
which implies that the interpreter's mind is not divisible, cannot
be in two places at once. Such doubling is not a matter of doubt
among students of literature, who know myriad examples of
self-multiplication within the boundaries of individual works.
When a writer puts on a mask for ironic effect, as in Swift's "A
Modest Proposal," the interpreter's mind must be in two places at
once as he entertains both the perspective of the modest proposer
and the perspective of Swift. In every ironic construction we
entertain two perspectives at once, and there is not, I think, any
rigid limitation on the number of perspectives we can entertain at
once. Similarly, when an interpreter emphatically rejects the
attitudes of a speaker or writer, he also adopts those attitudes in
order to reject them.

I have dwelt on meaning and significance because I believe this purely analytical distinction can help resolve some of the disagreements in hermeneutics, particularly certain disagreements involving the concept of historicity. This concept belongs to a third dimension of hermeneutics—the metaphysical. Adherents to Heidegger's metaphysics take the view that all attempts accurately to reconstruct past meanings are doomed to failure since not just our texts but also our understandings are historical. It is the nature of man to have no permanently defined nature distinct from his historically constituted existence. Whatever we know is decisively accommodated to our own historical world and cannot be known to us apart from that determining context. An interpreter must therefore learn to live with his historical self just as Freud would have him live with his subliminal self, not by trying to negate it, which is impossible, but by consciously making the best of it. Interpreters make the best of our historicity not by reconstructing an alien world from our texts but by interpreting them within our own world and making them speak to us.

*III*

This metaphysical position, skeptical and dogmatic at once, needs to be isolated from the analytical dimension of hermeneutics. No doubt it can be argued that analysis always carries metaphysical implications, and no doubt a shrewd ontologist could deduce metaphysical principles from the analytical distinction between meaning and significance. Yet I would wish to reply that the exercise would be pointless, since the distinction concords with a number of different metaphysical positions. Moreover, I would argue that there is far less danger in ignoring metaphysics than in introducing it prematurely into the practical questions of interpretation. A precocious ascent into the realm of ontology is just what needs to be avoided in the descriptive, analytical side of hermeneutic theory.

It is a notable irony that Heidegger's metaphysics itself depends upon a purely analytical principle taken directly from hermeneutic theory—namely the hermeneutic circle. This principle holds that the process of understanding is necessarily circular, since we cannot know a whole without knowing some of its constituent parts, yet we cannot know the parts as such without knowing the whole which determines their functions. (This principle can be easily grasped by self-consciously construing a sentence.) In *Sein und Zeit*, Heidegger expands the circumference of the hermeneutic circle beyond textual interpretation to embrace all knowing. Everywhere in knowledge the whole is prior to its parts, since the meaningfulness of a part is disclosed only in its relation to or function within a larger whole. The prior sense of the whole which ultimately lends meaning to any person's experience is his spiritual cosmos or *Welt*. But, since a person's *Welt* is always constitutively historical, it follows that any meaning we experience must have been pre-accommodated to our historical world. We cannot escape the fact that our historical world is a pre-given of our experience and is therefore constitutive of any textual interpretation.

This generalized version of the hermeneutic circle seems at first glance to support the position that accurate reconstruction of past meaning is impossible. It is futile to project ourselves into the historical past where our texts arose, since our own present world is already pre-given in our attempted projection. Our reconstruction can never be authentic because we can never exclude our own world, through which alone the past was disclosed. Our own present is the pre-given and the foregone conclusion in any historical reconstruction. If Heidegger's version of the hermeneutic circle is correct, it follows that the traditional aims of historical scholarship are largely illusory.

The direct application of this metaphysical argument to textual interpretation seems to me premature on at least two grounds. First, the metaphysical principle says nothing about subtle questions of degree. It argues that some degree of anachronism is necessarily present in any historical reconstruction, but as to whether a particular reconstruction is severely or trivially compromised the principle says nothing. The history of interpretation exhibits remarkable congruities between views of, say, *Hamlet* in the nineteenth and twentieth centuries, and shows remarkable conflicts of interpretation within the confines of either period. Obviously, the pre-given historical world cannot be the decisive factor that accounts in such cases for the similarities between different periods or the unreconcilable differences of interpretation within the same period. A premature recourse to metaphysics in order to explain these anomalies can easily become a facile substitute for serious thought, and historical reconstruction can cease to be even a plausible goal of inquiry. That is not, however, the logical consequence of Heidegger's metaphysics. Under his principles, all interpretations are time-bound and anachronistic, both those which attempt accurate reconstruction and those which do not. Yet deliberate reconstructions are different from deliberate anachronisms whether or not we follow Heidegger, and a particular reconstruction *may* be fairly accurate even under his principles. It follows that the decision to attempt a reconstruction instead of a vital, present-day interpretation is not, after all, governed by metaphysics. Even if Heidegger is right, the two kinds of attempt are both possible, and the decision to make one kind of attempt rather than the other remains an ethical choice, not a metaphysical necessity.

The second and more important objection to carrying Heidegger's metaphysics directly into the theory of interpretation is that his expanded version of the hermeneutic circle is in crucial respects probably wrong. The principle of the hermeneutic circle does not lead inevitably to dogmatic historical skepticism. If an interpretation is grounded in the interpreter's entire *Welt*, it will no doubt be different from any past meaning, since undoubtedly a person's entire spiritual world will be different from any that existed in the past. Yet it is open to question whether the whole that prestructures meaning must be conceived in this comprehensive way. The very introduction of "historicity" as a chief characteristic of *Welt* means that a boundary has been drawn, since historicity is not the chief component of a person's spiritual world. It is, rather, a limited domain of shared cultural experience apart from the bigger domain of unshared experience that makes up a person's world. The Heideggerian concept of *Welt* is at times undistinguishable from what used to be called *Zeitgeist*, and is just as problematical as the earlier concept. To limit the circumference of *Welt* (after having insisted upon its expansion) at the vague boundary between shared and private experience is entirely arbitrary.

Nevertheless, a boundary is certainly convenient. For if *Welt* is taken in its entirety, then each person's *Welt* is unique, and accurate understanding of another's meaning becomes impossible. But if I agree to draw a boundary, how do I decide where it should be drawn? I see only one way to avoid arbitrariness in the decision, and it is based on the observation that the *Welt* which actively prestructures an interpretation is always a highly selective sub-cosmos of an interpreter's world. For instance, any person who is now understanding my present discourse must be *excluding* far more of his spiritual world than ever he is bringing to the exercise. Such excluding is indeed logically necessary to any act of interpretation. On logical grounds, De Morgan has brilliantly shown that we cannot interpret discourse without limiting the *Welt* or "universe" that forms its context, and he coined the phrase "universe of discourse" to describe this necessary limitation.[4] Since the spiritual universe that actively governs an interpretation is limited and selective, no inherent necessity requires this delimited world to be different from any that existed in the past.

This last objection to Heidegger's dogmatic historical skepticism is, I believe, fatal, but the implications of these objections for the theory and practice of interpretation are the matters I wish to stress, and these implications are to my mind bluntly negative on the question whether metaphysics offers anything of practical utility to hermeneutic theory. First, metaphysical speculation has not yet brought to interpretation the power to deduce, a priori, significant matters of fact. It does not demonstrate that fairly accurate reconstruction is impossible; it does not, to my mind, even prove that absolutely accurate reconstruction doesn't actually occur, for metaphysics has no power to legislate what is or is not the case in the realm of the possible.

It cannot, therefore, help us in specific instances. Second, meta-(2) physics, being by nature universal, applies indiscriminately to all interpretations, both those that attempt historical reconstruction and those that disdain it. Thus, it provides no basis for choice as between various aims of interpretation. Powerless in deciding matters of fact, Heideggerian metaphysics is equally powerless to dictate what ought to be chosen in the realm of values. We can depend neither on metaphysics nor on neutral analysis in order to make decisions about the goals of interpretation. We have to enter the realm of ethics. For, after rejecting ill-founded attempts to derive values and goals from the presumed nature of interpretation, or from the nature of Being, what really remains is ethical persuasion.

## IV

In resisting some claims of current "metaphysical hermeneutics" I must admit to at least one metaphysical assertion: an interpreter is not necessarily so trapped in historicity that he loses his freedom; he is free to choose his aims, and within the context of those aims and the broad conventions of language, he is free to choose his meanings. I therefore understand the current controversy over historicity as a conflict not of abstract theories, but of values. When we are urged to adopt present relevance rather than original meaning as the "best meaning," we find ourselves repeating the old pattern of controversy between the medieval allegorists (the Heideggerians of an earlier day) and the later humanists. While this conflict cannot be resolved by mere analysis, its issues can be clarified, and clarification may bring unforeseen agreement.

Sometimes, for instance, the conflict between proponents of original and of anachronistic meaning is shown by analysis to be no conflict at all. These arguments about meaning sometimes originate in a failure to notice that meaning and significance—two different things—are being given the same name. To take a homely and simple example, some time ago, while driving on the

New Jersey Turnpike, my wife and I were trying to interpret a
sign that kept appearing on the median strip of the highway. It
looked like this:

```
 ┌─────────────────────────┐
 │                         │
 │  )                 (    │
 │  ⌐                 ⌐    │
 │       1 0 0 0           │
 │                         │
 └─────────────────────────┘
```

After pondering these hieroglyphics in vain, we began to notice
a feature of the Turnpike that was consistently associated with
the sign; a few seconds after seeing the sign, we would pass a gap
in the median strip wide enough to let a car cross over to the
other side of the road. At this gap we found another sign:

```
 ┌─────────────────────────┐
 │                         │
 │   FOR OFFICIAL          │
 │   USE ONLY              │
 │                         │
 └─────────────────────────┘
```

The problem was solved. The mysterious sign foretold that a gap
would appear in the median strip after 1000 feet. But I was not
altogether satisfied with my wife's description of the sign's meaning, namely that "official cars will be able to turn onto the other
side of the road after 1000 feet."

   No one would deny that my wife's interpretation was justified. My only doubt was whether the interpretation described
the sign's *meaning*. While it certainly described a significance of
the sign to drivers of official cars and other law-abiding person-
alities, what about its significance to a bank robber who is
trying to elude official cars? Wouldn't he regard the sign as
signalling an opportunity to reverse his direction? What about a
stranded pedestrian or a theorist? Would they interpret the first
sign as meaning something about official cars?

```
 ┌─────────────────────────┐
 │                         │
 │  )                 (    │
 │  ⌐                 ⌐    │
 │       1 0 0 0           │
 │                         │
 └─────────────────────────┘
```

What would happen to the sign's meaning if the authorities
decided to take down all the secondary signs that restricted the

use of the gaps to official cars? In these imaginary instances, the mysterious sign would still preserve a stable, self-identical meaning, namely that a gap will occur in the median strip after 1000 feet.

I find this example instructive in a number of ways. It suggests, first of all, that meaning cannot exceed the conventional semantic *possibilities* of the symbols used. After all, nothing in the original sign restricts the meaning to official cars, although the following sign, for example, undoubtedly would:

Second, even if we wish to determine meaning according to the author's original intention, meaning still operates under the above constraint, because although the original intention was to restrict the sign's *application*, nothing in the symbol-system exhibits that restriction in a communicable way. Third, we can infer from the example that private or coterie symbol-systems lose their restrictiveness as soon as the code becomes known outside the coterie—in this case the closed society of officials on official highway business. Once the secret symbols have been interpreted for me, the sign means the same thing for me (not to-me) as it does to a highway patrolman or to anyone else who has learned the code. (*The Waste Land* was once a coterie poem; now it is understood by high school students.) Fourth, the distinction between the communicable meaning of the highway sign, or any other symbol-system and its various kinds of significance applies universally to authors and interpreters alike. Thus, while the original intention was no doubt to restrict the sign's application or audience, that does not alter its original communicable meaning, but simply defines its *original significance*, which is quite another matter.

For some time now literary theorists, particularly the New Critics, have attempted to preserve this distinction under a different guise, and have deplored the use of biographical or historical information for restricting textual meaning to its original historical or biographical circumstances. Even if Shakespeare had written *Richard II* to support the rebellion of Essex (which of course he didn't) that wouldn't limit the meaning of the play to its original application. When the followers of Essex brought out the play's significance to their political aims, however, no great violence was done to its original meaning. Nor would any important distortion result from documents that showed autobiographical impulses in Shakespeare's portrayal of Richard. Modern applications of Shakespeare's original meaning could be equally innocent of distortive influence. For a self-identical meaning (original or anachronistic, simple or complex) has the great advantage of flexibility; being very sure of itself, of its self-identity, it can enter new worlds and play new roles with confidence.

If one resists confusing meaning and significance, one gets the impression that most controversies in interpretation do not really involve a conflict over original meaning versus anachronistic meaning. Usually the debates can be readily transposed into disagreement over the proper *emphases* of an interpretation, over whether it is better to explain original meaning or to bring out some aspect of the significance of meaning, for the interpreter or for present-day readers. The followers of Essex took the second course, without necessarily distorting Shakespeare's meaning. Our imaginary bank robber on the New Jersey Turnpike would not be distorting the meaning of the highway sign if he decided to disregard its "official use" and found a special significance for himself. In examples like these, original meaning is tacitly assumed even while original significance is ignored. Whenever interpretive conflicts are concerned only with emphasis in the conduct of a commentary, then they are conflicts about immediate aims and not about meanings. Most interpreters retain a respect for original meaning, and recognition of this might mollify some of our disagreements.

No doubt, what I am saying could never bring together certain extreme controversialists like Roland Barthes and Raymond Picard who have recently acted out the old dilemmas of original versus anachronistic meaning in their polemics over Racine.

*none of the interpretations I involve*

*significance*

What can one say by way of reconciliation if Barthes claims to be uninterested in Racine's original meaning, and Picard argues that Racine could not have meant what Barthes construes from the texts? It is difficult for a non-specialist to judge the true facts of this noted case, but I have the impression that the controversy provides an unusually pure modern example of the rival claims between original and anachronistic meaning. Most recent conflicts between ancients like Picard and moderns like Barthes are not so clearly drawn, since most of us would be chagrined to learn that we had made elementary mistakes in construing the language of an early period, and our very embarrassment would indicate that we recognized the co-equal and harmonious claims of original meaning and modern significance, even if Barthes does not. At the same time, most interpreters would reject the opposite excess (even if Picard does not) of ignoring the difference between original meaning and original significance, an oversight that is the occupational vice of antiquarians. With excesses on both sides, Barthes and Picard can serve as a cautionary example, to help avoid a head-on collision between original meaning and anachronistic meaning. That much the analytical dimension of hermeneutics can serve to do.

But the ethical problem is not to be solved quite that simply. Even if some interpretive disagreements turn out to reside in choice of emphasis rather than choice of meaning, still a choice of emphasis is ultimately an ethical choice. Many of us have felt at one time or other a distinct preference for anachronistic over original meaning, although nothing in the analytical or metaphysical dimensions of hermeneutics compels us to choose one over the other. Even textual editors, who owe professional allegiance to the author's original meaning, have been known to waver. Should "Music when soft voices die" really stand as the first line of Shelley's poem? Should brightness really fall from the "hair" instead of from the "air"? The text sometimes seems so much better if we ignore the author's probable intention or what he probably wrote. Every interpreter has a touch of the medieval commentator looking for the best meaning, and every editor has a drop of Bentley's blood. It is not rare that anachronistic meaning on *some* ground or other is undoubtedly the best meaning.

Therefore, let me state what I consider to be a fundamental ethical maxim for interpretation, a maxim that claims no privileged sanction from metaphysics or analysis, but only from general ethical tenets, generally shared. *Unless there is a powerful overriding value in disregarding an author's intention (i.e., original meaning), we who interpret as a vocation should not disregard it.* Mere individual preference would not be such an overriding value, nor would be the mere preferences of many persons. The possible exception is mentioned only because every ethical maxim requires such an escape clause. (Example: unless there is a powerful overriding value in lying, a person should tell the truth. Yet there are times when a lie is ethically better than to tell the truth, so the maxim cannot be an absolute one.) Similarly, one might fudge on original meaning for the sake of young, impressionable children, and so on. But except in these very special cases there is a strong ethical presumption against anachronistic meaning. When we simply use an author's words for our own purposes without respecting his intention, we transgress what Charles Stevenson in another context called "the ethics of language," just as we transgress ethical norms when we use another person merely for our own ends. Kant held it to be a foundation of moral action that men should be conceived as ends in themselves, and not as instruments of other men. This imperative is transferable to the words of men because speech is an extension and expression of men in the social domain, and also because when we fail to conjoin a man's intentions to his words we lose the soul of speech, which is to convey meaning and to understand what is intended to be conveyed.

I am not impressed with the view that this ethical imperative of speech, to which we all submit in ordinary discourse, is not applicable to written speech or, in particular, to literary texts. No literary theorist from Coleridge to the present has succeeded in formulating a viable distinction between the nature of ordinary written speech and the nature of literary written speech. For reasons I shall not pause to detail in this place, I believe the distinction can never be successfully formulated, and the futility of attempting the distinction will come to be generally recognized. Moreover, if it is seen that there is no viable distinction between "literature" and other classifications of written speech, it will also come to be recognized that the ethics of language hold good in all uses of language, oral and written, in poetry as well as in philosophy. All are ethically governed by the intentions of the author. To treat an author's words merely as grist for one's own mill is ethically analogous to using another man merely for one's own purposes. I do not say such ruthlessness of interpretation is never justifiable in principle, but I cannot imagine an occasion where it would be justifiable in the professional practice of interpretation. The peculiarly modern anarchy of every man for himself in matters of interpretation may sound like the ultimate victory of the Protestant spirit. Actually, such anarchy is the direct consequence of transgressing the fundamental ethical norms of speech and its interpretation.

The question I always want to ask critics who dismiss authorial intention as their norm is one that could be transposed into the categorical imperative or simply into the golden rule. I want to ask them this: "When you write a piece of criticism, do you want me to disregard *your* intention and original meaning? Why do you say to me 'That is not what I meant at all; that is not it at all'? Why do you ask me to honor the ethics of language for your writings when you do not honor them for the writings of others?" It was not surprising that M. Barthes was displeased when his intentions were distorted by M. Picard. Few critics fail to show moral indignation when their meaning is distorted in reviews and other interpretations of their interpretations. But their sensitivity is often one-way, and in this they show an inconsistency amounting to a double standard—one for their authors, another for themselves. They are like the tenant farmer whose belief in redistributing everybody's property extended to land, money, horses, chickens, and cows, but, when asked about pigs, said: "Aw hell, you know I gotta couple of pigs."

The vocation of interpretation has always carried ethical duties. Recently, we have been reminded by Frederick Crews and others of the responsibilities that devolve on us because interpretation always implies ideology, and is thus never entirely removed from social action. (He who is not with me is against me.) We can add that a professional interpreter has an obligation to shared knowledge as well as to other social values, and that shared knowledge implies a shared norm of interpretation. But aside from these public responsibilities, an interpreter, like any other person, falls under the basic moral imperative of speech, which is to respect an author's intention. That is why, in ethical terms, original meaning is the "best meaning."

# Part II

# The Valuative Dimension

# 6
# Evaluation as Knowledge

Descriptive and normative judgments have ever been intertwined in criticism and literary theory. (The same is true of most intellectual activities, including mathematics.) Historically, this state of affairs has raised two separate questions in literary theory: (1) On what grounds is it true to say that value is an essential property of literature, and that valuation is therefore an essential element of description? (2) What, if any, are the normative criteria which, when applied to literature, will yield not only definitive evaluations but also accurate descriptions? Although the second question has consumed much theoretical energy in the recent past, I believe it is true that no judicial criteria can yield either definitive evaluations or accurate descriptions. It is well, therefore, to keep the questions separate. In this paper I shall be concerned with the first question; it has been receiving renewed attention, as recent essays by Mr. Krieger and Mr. Frye attest.[1] The contribution I shall try to make to the discussion is a technical one in which I shall be recalling some pertinent observations of Immanuel Kant.

The main point at issue between Mr. Frye and Mr. Krieger is the long-standing controversy between the separatists and the anti-separatists—between those who wish to separate the serious study of literature from mere ideology or taste, and those who find the attempt undesirable or philosophically naive. Most contemporary critics have taken a stand, if only implicitly, on one side or the other, and on this point Mr. Krieger is right to place me in the school of Frye. Yet the position of Mr. Krieger and the anti-separatists is, I believe, sound, with respect to some aspects of the problem, and in this chapter I shall be particularly concerned to explore those aspects. I hope that the exercise will help diminish disagreement over the issue.

The goal of Mr. Frye and the separatists is to isolate literary study from the vagaries of changing tastes so that, purged of these variable elements, the descriptive side of criticism will come into relief. Literary study will then take its proper place among the progressive disciplines of learning; it will aspire to the condition of science. In his "Polemical Introduction" Frye had the courage to speak of a "scientific element in criticism" and the rhetorical wisdom to caution "readers for whom the word 'scientific' conveys emotional overtones of unimaginative barbarism [that] they may substitute 'systematic' or 'progressive' instead."[2] Although Frye mistakenly equated "scientific" with an all-encompassing scheme of classification instead of with a critical testing of hypotheses, that did not diminish the force of his demand that literary description be purged of arbitrary evaluation. For if the ups and downs of the literary stock exchange are integral to literary study, then farewell progress, farewell genuine knowledge.

The anti-separatists, on the other side, have answered that all criticism, including Frye's, is larded with value judgments and that no one should *want* to divorce description from valuation: "What is the point of a fugitive and cloistered study which, under the pretext of scientism, disregards the very knowledge that is peculiarly appropriate to literature? The undertaking would signal a regression into that literary positivism and pseudo-scientific methodology against which the whole modern movement in literary scholarship has rightly rebelled. If the price of system and progress in the humanities is the exclusion of everything peculiarly humane, then the price is not worth paying. In any case, the alternatives are not so grim as that. Genuine knowledge of literature is possible, and it necessarily includes knowledge of values."

So much for metaphysical pathos. The question whether value judgments must adhere to the description of literature is not in itself solved by taking sides on the relative desirability of different critical procedures. Both sides have stated the problem as a theoretical issue, and it is a problem that is amenable to theoretical solution: Value description must adhere to literary description if, and only if, literature possesses ineluctable value as part of its essence. The theoretical argument against separatism is therefore stated cogently and in its proper terms by René Wellek:

> We cannot comprehend and analyze any work of art without reference to values. The very fact that I recognize a certain structure as "a work of art" implies a judgment of value. The error of pure phenomenology is in the assumption that such a dissociation is possible, that values are superimposed on structure, "inhere" on or in structures.[3]

Any accurate descriptions of literary works must therefore have reference to the values that make them literature and not another thing. And description of value is evaluation; to separate the two is an ontological impossibility. Wellek is very explicit: we cannot even *comprehend* a work of art as in itself it really is without at the same time making a judgment of value. This assertion is worth wrestling with at the most serious level, and seriousness requires one to ask first what "value" in such a context means or ought to mean.

The word "value" is sometimes used as if it represented an independent reality like a rock or a piece of gold. Yet nobody has ever seen or imagined a value as an independent reality. Something that "has value" must be actually or potentially worth something to somebody in some respect; outside of that relationship, it cannot have that value. No doubt some things are valuable in certain respects to human beings generally, but this hardly bestows on us the right to speak of such value relationships in absolute terms.

> While Man exclaims "See all things for my use!"
> "See man for mine" replies a pamper'd goose.

Value as such, absolute value, would be value-to-God, and even in this ultimate, presumptuous judgment the concept would still be relational and specific: valuable to God in what respects? The words "value" and "valuable" considered apart from such relationships correspond to nothing that exists or could exist. This view is often called an "instrumentalist" conception of value, and, while I prefer the adjective "relational" to "instrumental," I accept it as being the only conception which, in my knowledge

of the subject, corresponds to reality. That the conception is
perfectly adequate for dealing with aesthetic and other values
found in literature has been argued convincingly by Monroe
Beardsley.[4]

Yet despite this caveat, which would lead to some modifi-
cations in Wellek's phrasing, I believe he is right to say that a
literary work "is a totality of values which do not adhere to the
structure but constitute its very nature. All attempts to drain
value from literature have failed and will fail because its very
essence is value."[5] An instrumentalist would, of course, want to
ask Wellek how literary value (which must reside in the relationships between a work and its readers) could at the same time
constitute the work's "very essence." The hardheaded instrumentalist position would seem to require a qualification of Wellek's claim, since for an instrumentalist *nothing* could have value
as part of its essence. Yet I believe that the two views are
reconcilable, and, moreover, that the process of reconciling
them will solve one of the knottier problems of critical theory.

The problem is essentially the one which Kant confronted in
his *Critique of Judgment.* The crucially important element in
Kant's theory for the issue at hand is not his definition of
aesthetic value, but rather his argument for the objectivity of
such value. For Kant as for Wellek, value is conceived as belonging to the very essence of a work of art:

> If one declares something to be beautiful ... he judges not
> solely for himself, but for everyone, and then speaks of beauty
> as if it were a property of things. Hence he says the *thing*
> is beautiful.[6]

The aesthetic value of anything cannot be dissociated from the
thing itself as an object of aesthetic contemplation. Thus, Kant
ends the *Analytic of the Beautiful* with the sentence: "The beautiful is that which is recognized without concepts to be the object
of a *necessary* delight." For the anti-separatists everything depends upon whether this position can be successfully upheld. If
so, it must follow that no description of literature can properly
escape judgments of value, since Kant's argument about beauty
would apply to all the values which belong to the work as a
necessary property of its being perceived.

Kant is properly solicitous to preserve the relational character of beauty even while he argues for its ineluctability, thereby meeting the requirement that any value, including that of beauty, must be relational. A beautiful object is inherently beautiful because it is or ought to be universally beautiful to mankind. For the experience of beauty is subjective; its "objectivity" consists in the universality of the subjective experience:

> Such universality is not an objective, but only a subjective quantity of judgment . . . a subjective universal validity. . . . Precisely for this reason, the aesthetic universality ascribed to a judgment must be of a special kind. For it does not connect the predicate of beauty with the concept of the object in its entire logical sphere, yet nevertheless extends it over the whole sphere of judging subjects. (sec. 8)

This concept of a necessary and therefore universal subjective judgment of value has been a stumbling block to modern readers of Kant, for whom the differences of subjective values among men have seemed more noticeable than the similarities. Everything we have learned since the great historicist revolution which gathered force in Kant's lifetime has confirmed us in our skepticism toward the idea of a common human nature. Yet Kant is quite explicit in stating that some such idea is required to uphold the theory of necessary value: "Only under the presupposition of a common sense does it become possible to make a necessary judgment of value."[7] As a modern writer, Mr. Wellek, naturally enough, eschews this exigency by speaking of values as though they had independent objectivity instead of subjective universality, but for an instrumentalist, Kant's position must be considered the right one. The crucial point is that the observable variations in our subjective value judgments do not affect Kant's profound argument in defense of "objective" values. For he openly concedes that individual tastes are variable :

> Violet is a soft and lovely color to one person, cold and dead to another. One man loves the sound of wind instruments, another that of strings. It would be folly to quarrel over such matters and to condemn judgments differing from ours as incorrect. (sec. 7)

To grant this much from the start, Kant must have in view some very powerful arguments for a common sense among mankind and the necessary value judgments it entails. If his arguments hold (and I believe that they do), then Wellek's insistence on the inseparability of literary description and evaluation must be correct.

The easiest and most direct way to defend the concept of necessary value would be to argue that a poem or other work of art cannot be perceived (in Wellek's term "comprehended") except as an object of value. The value of the work would then be part of the cognition itself. Yet this direct line of argument is vulnerable, since the necessary value to us of something we perceive (its beauty to us, for example) can be realized only *after* we have perceived it. If we try to make a value judgment before having cognized the object, the best we can say is: "This experience is giving me pleasure." But we could not impute a universal validity to the value judgment, since it would not be grounded in something universally sharable, namely the cognition of the work. Early in the *Analytic* Kant devotes a long section to the question whether a judgment of value "is prior to or posterior to cognizing the object," commenting that "the solution to this problem is the key to the critique of taste" (sec. 9). His answer is straightforward:

> Nothing can be universally communicated and shared except cognition and representation in so far as it belongs to cognition. For only in so far as it belongs to cognition is representation objective and has a universal point of reference with which everyone's faculty of representation is obliged to tally. (sec. 9)

Kant's insistence on the priority of cognition is therefore a logical inference about the relationship of cognition to necessary judgments of value; it is not an empirical description of psychic events. Within this limitation the argument is compelling.

It is not yet clear, however, why Kant should have considered this point the key to the critique of taste, particularly since his defense of necessary value judgments must depend not on the priority of cognition but on the existence of a universal common sense. The two issues turn out to be intimately connected. Behind his formidable facade, Kant is often a great ironist and a great dramatist of ideas. He has carefully erected all the major obstacles to his goal in order to show that the obstacles themselves will become the high road to his conclusions. He has conceded that judgments of beauty are subjective: further, that necessary subjective judgments require a universally shared object of cognition and a universally shared subjectivity (common sense). Yet he has also conceded that subjective value preferences are highly variable. The *peripeteia* and *anagnorisis* of this intellectual drama occur at the end of the *Analytic* when Kant proves that *a common sense is required not merely for a universal subjective judgment but also for a cognition of the object itself.* That is why the priority of cognition is the key not only to the critique of taste but also to the problem addressed in this essay. Kant has provided, I believe, the only possible grounds for asserting the inseparability of literary description and value judgment, and is quite justified in maintaining that his solution is "worthy of the greatest attention" (sec. 9).

His argument is in many ways analogous to that of the first *Critique.* There one of his goals had been to defend the objectivity of scientific knowledge, just as here he defends the objectivity of aesthetic judgment, but in this case, instead of being forced back to the most abstract and primary categories of experience, he is stopped short in a domain which requires the application of cultural categories to the facts of cultural experience. Kant's procedure shows very clearly that it was he and not the twentieth-century phenomenologists who first conceived the value-laden objects of cultural experience as epistemological ultimates. It was he, not ourselves, who first discovered the irreducible connection of "fact" and "value" in the *Lebenswelt.* For Kant argues that the objects of cultural experience, no less than those of primary sensation, are constituted by the mental organization of the perceiver. "The eye altering alters all." The object of cognition, when we perceive a flower, a poem, a painting is in itself constituted by the "mental set" we adopt to perceive it. If we are to have a shared cultural object of cognition, we must also have a "common sense" with respect to that object.

Thus, at the end of the *Analytic* Kant rests his case for inherently necessary value judgments on the fact that our very cognition of a shared cultural object presupposes a shared system of feelings and attitudes with respect to it:

> If cognitions must be able to be shared, then that mental state in which the cognitive powers are attuned for cognition must also be able to be shared. And in particular that proportion or ratio of the cognitive powers that is required to turn a representation (by which an object is given us) into knowledge must be able to be shared. For this ratio [i.e., "mental set"] is the subjective condition of knowing, and without it knowledge as an effect could not arise. (sec. 21)

Kant's theme being the judgment of beauty, he defines the mental set narrowly as "a harmony of the mental powers," but his argument holds by implication for any other sort of value judgment. This should be kept in mind in following the next stage of his argument when he connects a shared cognition not only to a shared mental set but also, necessarily, to a shared feeling:

> There must be one harmony in which in the inner ratio is most propitious to the quickening of mental powers for the purpose of cognition, and this harmony can be discovered in no other way than by feeling. . . . Now this harmony itself must be able to be universally shared [otherwise the object could not be] and consequently also the feeling of it on the occasion of a given representation. (sec. 21)

To deny this chain of reasoning would be equivalent to denying the possibility of any sort of knowledge:

> It follows that there is a good reason for assuming a common sense. And we can do so without resting our case on psychological observations. Rather, we assume a common sense as the necessary condition without which knowledge could

not be shared universally; and this is a possibility that is pre-supposed in every logic and every principle of knowledge that is not sceptical. (sec. 21)

By refusing to separate value preferences from the mental set required in certain types of cognition, Kant has made it impossible to separate value judgments from the cognition of art. His refusal seems to me altogether valid. For example, the degree to which some element in a poem receives emphasis in our experience of it will be partly determinant of its structure for us, partly determinant of what it *is* in our cognition of it. At the same time, the imposition of emphasis implies a judgment about relative importance—importance to us as well as to the poem since the poem for us is our cognition of it. But the judgment of relative importance is entirely an adjunct of the mental set adopted in a particular cognition, and is inseparable from the feeling which accompanies that particular kind of importance.

Kant's stress on feeling in subjective value judgments is thus eminently justified, and is a welcome antidote to the circumspectness with which nowadays we invoke vague, hypostatized entities called "values." Modern linguists and literary theorists do, of course, speak of "affective meanings" in contradistinction to "cognitive meanings." But how these two kinds of meanings relate to one another, or how indeed there could be such an entity as an affective *meaning* has not so far been satisfactorily explained.[8] Kant solves the problem by showing why cognitive meaning (the only kind there could be) is in most utterances accompanied by necessary affects in our cognition of it. The correlation of cognition and mental set makes this inevitable, and completely obviates the need for recourse to such a mysterious entity as affective meaning. Moreover, the correlation of cognition and necessary affect in experiencing literature is very much a part of what we mean in speaking of "literary values." For in addition to whatever social and ethical value literature may have, much of its special value to us must be of the kind which carries "subjective universal validity" and is inseparable from feeling.

The implications, however, of this necessary union between "fact" and "value" in literature cannot be altogether congenial to the anti-separatist position as it is usually formulated. The Kantian argument does not support a necessary union of description and evaluation as those terms are usually understood. When Kant's argument is translated into terms specifically appropriate to verbal works of art, it becomes an argument for the inseparability of *meaning* and value, and it takes the following form: The meaning of a literary work can be cognized only by adopting the specific mental set which is constitutive of that meaning. In relation to that mental set, the meaning will necessarily be accompanied by specific subjective value judgments. Since the relationship between the meaning and the subjective attitudes which constitute it is ineluctable, so therefore is the relationship between the meaning and the universal subjective value judgments which it sponsors. For example, we might read the following as a somewhat resentful accusation:

> Thou, silent form, dost tease us out of thought
> As doth eternity: Cold Pastoral!

If so, the meaning of the lines must be associated with a momentary diminishment of our exalted admiration for the Grecian urn and the consolation it brings. If, on the other hand, the words "tease" and "cold" are understood not as correlative to an attitude of resentment, but rather to a sense of still greater exaltation which transcends "all breathing human passion," then the feeling of admiration is not diminished or qualified but accentuated. Or, to suggest still another possibility, the words "tease" and "cold" might carry meanings correlative to more complex feelings, negative in some respects, emphatically positive in others. In each of these cases, *the cognitive meanings of the words would be just as different as their correlative affects.* And, more to the point, the different meanings could have *existence* only through the different constitutive mental sets which sponsored both the meanings and their correspondent affects.

This brings us to a problem which Kant omitted to consider.

Which of the various possible meanings attachable to Keats's lines is the one which carries "universal subjective validity" and therefore necessary value? One correct answer would be that each of these meanings carries its own necessary value, but this answer does not satisfy the requirement set by Kant and Wellek that the value be judged "as a property of the thing," not of one individual's perception of the thing. "Universal subjective validity" requires that the correctness (universal sharability) of the cognition be established, not just the correlation between cognition and value. Kant passes over this problem with the observation that "there must be one harmony in which this inner ratio is the most propitious to the mutual quickening of the mental powers for the purpose of cognition" (sec. 21). In other words, Kant's criterion for the correct cognition of a beautiful thing is that under it the thing becomes the most beautiful, the harmonious quickening of the mental powers the greatest. But, obviously, this criterion will serve only so long as beauty is the value being sought. If the most beautiful meaning (in Kant's sense) happens not to be the meaning intended by the author (as it would not be in, say, one of Tolstoy's late stories), then the problem of arbitrariness arises. The whole ground of "necessary value" would be destroyed, since the necessity rests entirely on a shared object of cognition. "Only in so far as it belongs to cognition is representation objective and has a universal point of reference with which everyone's faculty of representation is obliged to tally" (sec. 9).

It could be argued, of course, that the shared object of cognition (Tolstoy's story) is the same for everyone who adopts the aesthetic mental set defined by Kant. But even as an imaginative exercise this procedure would not carry the universal imperative originally demanded, since the aesthetic stance would not be "the one most propitious" to a cognition of Tolstoy's meanings. An implicit conflict would persist between Tolstoy's meanings and the ones realized by a purely aesthetic mode of contemplation. This is a crucial weakness in Kant's argument. With a work of art, the only object of cognition having implicit claim to be "a universal point of reference" is the sharable object cognized by its maker. The claim of privilege for any other object would be too arbitrary to carry genuine universality. The only values which can be considered intrinsic properties of a work of art are those which attach by subjective necessity to a re-cognition of the author's work.

This conclusion is altogether consistent with Wellek's assertion that "we cannot comprehend and analyze any work of art without reference to values." It also causes us to recognize a distinction between the different kinds of value judgment present in literary commentary. Some are intrinsic and necessary; some are not. The values which adhere by necessity to a description of meaning are those which subsist between the meaning and the subjective attitudes which constitute it. In other words, the only unavoidable judgments of value in literary commentary are those which are necessarily implied in interpretation. An interpretation of meaning cannot eschew the value judgments which are correlative to meaning; one cannot perform an ontological impossibility. On the other hand, it is quite possible to eschew other kinds of value judgment in literary commentary, although one should not avoid responsibility by doing so. I shall conclude this essay by showing that these other kinds of value judgment have as much inherent claim to genuine knowledge as the necessary value judgments implicit in interpretation.

The only universally valid cognition of a work of art is that which is constituted by the kind of subjective stance adopted in its creation. The value judgments correlative to that kind of mental set are thereby given in the very act of cognition. But other attitudes toward the work are obviously possible, both on the part of the critic and on the part of the author himself when critically judging his own work. On the surface this would seem to raise a problem for the Kantian schema, since the work can have existence only through the subjective stance which constitutes it; to interpret it from another stance would be to cognize another, different work. But this is not necessarily what happens. The judicial critic and the self-critical author can judge the work from an alien stance without relinquishing the privileged subjective stance which constitutes the work's meaning. A ready example of this simultaneous empathy and alienation is found in our experience of drama. In *Oedipus Rex* we understand from Oedipus' own point of view what he says about ridding Thebes of its plague, and at the same time we *judge* what he says from a quite different standpoint. It would be inaccurate to say that we interpret Oedipus' words differently from the way he meant them; the effect of Sophocles' irony depends upon our interpreting Oedipus' words precisely as he meant them and at the same time passing a judgment upon that meaning. Irony, whether verbal or dramatic, always entails this simultaneous adoption of two different mental sets, neither stance being assimilated to the other.

I choose an example from drama rather than from another form because in drama, even for purposes of pure interpretation, we must entertain at least two standpoints: that of the character who speaks and that of the playwright who (unbeknownst to the character) is controlling the significance of what he says. In principle there is no reason why this encompassing of one subjective stance by another could not continue indefinitely—the character's meaning judged and encompassed by that of the playwright, and both of these judged and encompassed by a critic. (I recently read an essay criticizing a critique of Johnson's criticism of Shakespeare's comedies.) The crucial point is that the application of an alien subjective stance does not necessarily destroy or distort the subjective stance which constitutes the meaning of a work. The integrity of the work with its attendant values can be preserved while judgment is passed upon it. Indeed, if this primordial integrity is not preserved, a critical judgment could not be valid, since the object criticized could no longer be "a universal point of reference with which everyone's faculty of representation is obliged to tally."

The example of drama points to another characteristic of literary evaluation which is crucial to its status as a form of knowledge. Nearly everyone would agree that the playwright's implicit judgment upon the speeches of his characters is an essential part of a play's meaning. But if this kind of critical judgment is granted an objective status in our knowledge of literature, there is no inherent reason why a critic's judgment of the playwright's work should not in turn be granted a similarly objective status. To qualify as objective knowledge, judicial evaluation need fulfill only two criteria: (1) that it be a judgment about the work and not about a distorted version of it, and (2) that the judgment be accurate with respect to the criteria applied. When Plato judges that Priam's appeal to Achilles is bad literature because it encourages men to act in an undignified manner, his judgment is correct on that criterion if (and only if) that is indeed the effect which Homer's description has. If a critic announces that literary excellence resides in the perfect correlation of a work's style with the ethos of the age when it was written, then any work which has this quality will also have literary excellence—on that criterion. Judgments that are accurately made upon explicit criteria furnish the grounds of their own validation and therefore qualify as knowledge. Of course, arguments about the relative merits of the various judicial criteria in literary criticism are another matter. These arguments cannot be resolved absolutely, but only with reference to further criteria (about which the disputants may or may not agree) regarding the proper functions of literature and criticism. It nevertheless remains true that accurate judicial evaluations made under explicitly chosen criteria have as much objectivity as accurate interpretations.

This analysis has led, therefore, to the following conclusions:

1. The interpretation (description) of a literary work is necessarily correlative to the particular subjective stances which constitute its meanings.

2. Affects and value judgments necessarily subsist in the relationship between meanings and these correlative subjective stances. These value judgments are therefore inherent in literary description.

3. Judicial criticism encompasses this unity of meaning, stance, and value by an alien (sometimes hostile) stance which can nevertheless preserve the integrity of the primordial one.

4. From this alien standpoint, new judgments of value and

significance can be predicated which are just as objective as pure description.

Finally, I should like to add a fifth conclusion which has been implicit throughout the analysis. The ascription of inherent value to a literary work of art is made possible by Kant's insight into the necessary subjective component that constitutes any shared cultural object. So far as I am aware, this Kantian insight provides the *only* grounds for ascribing necessary value to a literary work of art. Yet Kant's principle by no means limits itself to literature or works of art in general. If it holds at all, it must hold for any cultural object whatever, and emphatically for any use of language. A technical essay, an ordinary conversation, or a poem has, therefore, necessary, inherent values; of course, the values are different, but the structure of the argument for their existence is the same. It follows that there is no sound reason for isolating literature and art in a mysterious ontic realm apart from other cultural realities. The inherent values of literature are not thereby protected, but called into question by being made the objects of a mystique. Humane studies are best served by welcoming, not deploring the fact that the values of literature are continuous with all other shared values of human culture.

# 7
# Privileged Criteria in Evaluation

How well a literary work fulfills particular criteria of excellence is not easily decided, but is at least decidable. If critics are able to agree upon their criteria, they can also agree, and often do, in their specific evaluative judgments. More often, however, critics find themselves applying different norms with the result that some of the most vigorous debates in practical and theoretical criticism are those which concern the proper choice of criteria. But is there any proper choice of criteria in literary evaluation? Is it possible to demonstrate the inherent superiority of one evaluative mode over another? In short, do privileged literary criteria exist? If they do not, it must follow that no truly definitive value judgment can be pronounced upon any literary work.

When David Hume granted that no specific criteria of literary judgment could be "fixed by reasonings a priori,"[1] he was able to recommend instead an institutional criterion founded upon experience: a literary work should be deemed excellent which mankind has long judged to be so, or which the intellectual aristocracy of the present day judges to be so. Hume placed his confidence in the uniformity of human nature and the observable consensus among well-educated men. Good judges could be depended upon to agree that Addison is better than Bunyan.[2] Hume's pragmatic canon may be called "institutional" because, like all institutions, its authority rests upon social agreement. Just as legal pragmatists define correct judgment institutionally as the majority rule of the Supreme Court, Hume implicitly defined it as the majority rule of the best judges. In Hume's day the best judges could be recognized and accepted; implicitly they could be institutionalized on the analogy of the Supreme Court, the French Academy, or the Pope.

Sheer authority has always played a role in literary judgment, but the institutions in which it has resided have become constantly more diffuse and weak. Aristotle's rules gave way to the Humean consensus, which, in turn, gave way to the modern fragmentation of all traditional jurisdictions. Yet anyone who questions traditional authority is thrown back upon his own standards of taste, just as Luther, in questioning papal authority, was thrown back upon his own inward judgment in matters of faith. For some centuries now we have all been literary protestants without Pope or priesthood. Prophets and sects we continue to have, like the other Protestants, but nothing resembling a Pope or a Supreme Court. Matthew Arnold's admiration for the French Academy was wistful and half-hearted, as though he foresaw the collapse of its authority in modern times. His idea of substituting an inward Academy in the minds and hearts of Englishmen was just another retreat into the pervasive literary protestantism.[3]

Coleridge, coming between Hume and Arnold, saw very clearly these analogies between the sources of authority in religion, in law, and in literature. Authority is normally derived from socially accepted institutions, and when the institutions are endangered, new grounds of authority have to be provided. In this perspective, Coleridge's literary theories have the same philosophical and social motivation as his writings upon church and state. For Coleridge, judicial authority in all cultural domains must henceforth be deduced by necessity from the nature of the cosmos and the human mind. The new, intrinsic system of authority thus derived would be independent of mere prophetic revelation on the one side and accidental social development on the other. Everywhere, perforce, the model of excellence would be the pattern of the God-infused cosmos: the unity of all in each; just as everywhere the model of disvalue would be the contrary of the divine plan: disconnection, dead and spiritless. Thus, in literary judgment, all criteria of excellence may be comprised in the principle of organic unity, the reconciliation of opposite and discordant qualities.

Coleridge's was the most significant attempt in criticism to erect a comprehensive philosophical substitute for the fallen edifice of literary authority. Mankind could no longer depend upon the dispersed and discredited Humean consensus; unless "the reviewers support their decisions by reference to fixed canons of criticism, previously established and deduced from the nature of man, reflecting minds will pronounce it arrogance in them thus to announce themselves to men of letters as the guides of their taste and judgment."[4] Every decision must show its credentials; predilection must give way to principle.

This great program failed (as all similar ones have) for two equally instructive reasons. First, Coleridge's great root principle, deduced from the nature of man and the cosmos, was impossibly general, so that he was frequently unable to correlate his particular evaluative criteria with his universal principle. Because much that he found excellent in literature could not be reduced to the cosmological archetype, he had the good sense (against his announced program) not to attempt the reduction. Second, he failed because the philosophical deduction of critical canons proved to be no more self-evident or self-confirming than the arbitrary canons of the petulant reviewers. The great underlying principle which had generated the new philosophical canons of criticism could not itself command adherence unless one happened to share Coleridge's belief in an organic, God-infused cosmos where each thing has a life of its own and we are all one life.[5] Coleridge's deduction required a prior commitment from the general reader which was no less arbitrary than the prior commitment to shared values required by the ordinary reviewer. In Coleridge's system, more—not less—reliance was placed upon a higher, *ab extra* revelation, and the new religion, upon which all depended, became merely one more sect among other literary sects. Despite Coleridge's grand, catholic effort, literary protestantism held its inevitable sway.

In our own, still more fragmented era, further efforts have been made to solve the problem which Coleridge so clearly perceived. Since there is no papacy in intellectual affairs, the definitive judgment of literary value will have to come from principle, not authority. And the principle will have to be one which can rightly claim a preferential status in relation to other evaluative principles. Thus, a great deal of effort in recent literary theory has been directed to the deduction of evaluative criteria which can be shown to have this privileged status. The throne of vanished authority will be occupied by a supreme jurisdiction mightier far than that which we have lost. Through it, we shall be able at last to make permanently valid judgments of literary value. No longer the nightmare of protestantism—graceless zealots fighting over modes of faith; ultimately we shall establish a new universal criticism founded upon the inherent nature of literature itself.

This modern strategy was the only one left which gave promise of success. In the absence of an instituted authority or a *consensus didacti*, the only possible way to secure a privileged status for evaluative criteria would be to deduce them from the nature of literature itself. Literature would have to be judged as literature, poetry as poetry, and not referred to some alien standard. Self-evidently, such a judgment would be more definitive than an evaluation based upon social utility, arbitrary rules, or personal taste. To judge literature as literature and not another thing would be to reach a determination independent of shifting opinions and tides of taste, for the judgment would be made upon intrinsic grounds. Other modes of evaluation would continue to be made on other premises, but they would remain merely relative judgments, dependent upon external and changeable value preferences. Intrinsic evaluation, on the other hand, would be permanent and secure, privileged and immutable, because the grounds of judgment would be derived from the very nature of the thing judged.

Aristotle had done the thing before, and, in his own way, so had Coleridge. But the motto "literature as literature" was in itself no protection against internecine warfare between those who adopted it. In fact, the most vigorous polemics in recent critical theory arose between the Chicago critics and the New Haven critics who shared the same revolutionary goal of deposing extrinsic scholarship in favor of intrinsic criticism; the Mensheviks were embattled against the Bolsheviks over the true method of the revolution, and only the vigor of their conflict suffced to mask the structural identity of their aim. No matter if Aristotle or if Coleridge was taken to be the true prophet of the revolution, its goal was conceived by both parties to be the criticism of "literature as literature."

Despite the important benefits which have accrued to us in the domain of interpretive analysis by virtue of this critical revolution, polemics and failure were its inevitable fruits in the domain of evaluation. For the goal of a definitive, literary evaluation of literature is actually a mirage masked by a tautology. The ideal of a privileged "literary" mode of evaluation is rendered hopeless by the impossibility of deducing genuinely privileged, literary criteria of evaluation. I make this statement categorically, because an analysis of the various types of evaluative principles which have evolved in the history of criticism reveals that such criteria have never been successfully formulated, and, in the nature of the case, never could be.

Broadly speaking, four principal modes of literary evaluation have evolved in the history of criticism, and in their basic structures these four modes would seem to exhaust the possibilities.[6] Of course, any such scheme of classification will oversimplify the subject matter and will serve to indicate only the underlying logic of the problem rather than the richness of the various solutions that have been proposed. For in actuality, all good critics and theorists have adopted more than one of the four strategies. Thus, when I attach a particular historical name to one of them, I am suggesting a preponderant emphasis rather than formulating an adequate description. Nonetheless, each strategy retains its characteristic features, whether viewed in isolated purity or in admixture with others, so that if conclusions can be reached about the relative merits of each, it will be possible to decide which strategy, if any, occupies a privileged position.

The first type of evaluative theory I would call extrinsic, since it ruthlessly decides whether a work of literature is good or bad on the grounds of its external relationships. The great example is, of course, Plato. His line of argument is beautifully consistent and rigorous. A work of literature shall be judged good if and only if it is good for the state. What is good for the state is to be defined thus and thus, and what is bad thus and thus. Those elements in literature which conduce to bad effects should be censored or at least censured. Tolstoy is another of these ruthless extrinsic critics, and although very few men have had the courageous if not perverse rigor of a Plato or a Tolstoy, a number of very great critics, Johnson and Arnold for example, have practiced a measure of extrinsic evaluation. I. A. Richards once made the remark that if the extrinsic critics were to be lined up against the intrinsic ones, all the best brains would be found on the side of Plato.[7] That is a point to which I shall revert at the end of this chapter.

The fountainhead of the second type of theory is Aristotle, the *(2)* father of evaluation-through-the-genre. A work shall be judged good to the extent that it fulfills the intrinsic imperatives of the kind to which it belongs, and it shall be judged bad to the extent that it fails to fulfill those generic imperatives. Each thing shall be judged not in relation to the state or some other external standard, but in relation to the proper criteria of the subsuming species. Thus, as the Chicago theorists have insisted, the right way to judge a comic novel is not according to universal or external literary criteria, but according to the criteria specifically appropriate to comic novels.

The third type of theory, which might be called individual- *(3)* istic, is Aristotle pushed to the extreme of nominalistic skepticism. True, the proper way to judge a work is according to its own intrinsic imperatives, but these cannot be defined in advance by reference to a limited number of genres and sub-genres. Every new work is *sui generis*. One has only to look at the history of literature to discover that Aristotle's norms of tragedy do not accurately define the norms of Shakespearean tragedy. And, in fact, the norms of *Hamlet* are not even identical with those of *King Lear*. The only system of criteria genuinely intrinsic to a work is the one defined by the particular goals of the work itself. The only privileged criterion, therefore, is adequacy: how fully does the work accomplish what it is trying to do; how expressive is it of its own intent? The word "expressive" should remind us that the most considerable representative of the individualistic theory is Croce.

(4)   Finally, the fourth type of theory is a well-represented one which embraces a large number of writers in the history of criticism. I call it the broad-genre theory. With Aristotle in the middle and Croce on the far right, these more liberal intrinsic critics want to comprise all or most of what we call literature within a single comprehensive class having certain common attributes and excellences. Under this theory the Aristotelian principle is extended over a much wider domain, so that instead of positing that all tragedy aspires to arouse and purge our pity and fear, one posits that all literature aspires to instruct and delight, or to achieve complexity, or to express the dream of man. Sometimes the broad class literature is narrowed, for example, to poetry and non-poetry, so that Coleridge in his version of the broad-genre theory defines the attributes of poetry in such a way that it embraces some passages of prose and excludes some passages of verse. Other broad-genre theorists, notably those who pursue the discipline of aesthetics, expand the confines of the subsuming species to include not just all literature but all art. But in every case, theorists of this persuasion determine their criteria of evaluation according to the intrinsic, Aristotelian pattern. They posit a species: literature, poetry, art; they define the proper excellence of that species in a generally applicable way; and they evaluate individual works according to the degree they fulfill that proper excellence.

What we have, then, in the history of criticism are four basic strategies for formulating criteria, three claiming to be intrinsic, and one being unabashedly extrinsic. The three intrinsic procedures are, as I have suggested, Aristotelian in their skeletal structure, so that the fundamental conflict goes back, very appropriately, to Plato versus Aristotle. That awesome thought should not deter us, however, from attempting an adjudication between them on this narrow issue of literary evaluation. Very briefly, and reversing the previous sequence, I shall review some of the problems that beset each type of evaluative procedure.

The broad-genre type of theory was very forcefully and (4)←
cogently criticized by the late Ronald Crane in his essay on
Cleanth Brooks and critical monism.[8] By critical monism Crane
meant, among other things, the iterative use of a single canon of
evaluation for all works of literature. Crane argued that the
universal application of a single criterion like irony or complexity inevitably ignored the primary aims and values which informed the work. Thus, on the universal criterion of irony, the
greatest poem of the twentieth century is Einstein's $E = mc^2$.

To Crane's objections regarding the inappropriateness of such
critical monism, it is possible to add another which is more
central to the present analysis. Broad-genre evaluation proffers
an implicit claim which it fails to make good. It claims a privileged status for its judgments because it evaluates literature as
literature. Its criteria claim to be intrinsic on the assumption that
all the works we call literature have in common certain implicit
aims. Yet this assumption has never been successfully defended,
and indeed it is false. The only occasion when a particular
criterion such as beauty, complexity, paradoxicality, maturity,
sincerity, and so forth, could be intrinsic to a work is when that
quality is in fact an intrinsic aim of the work. And since no such
quality is universally aimed at by all literary works, no such
criterion could be universally intrinsic. I do not mean to imply,
as Crane did, that there is something illegitimate in applying a
single criterion to all literary works. On the contrary, I shall, in
the end, defend its legitimacy. What I deny is the claim that such
criteria are intrinsic, that they could have a privileged status.
Broad-genre evaluation cannot do the job it pretends to do.
Since its criteria are *not* self-grounded in literature, it cannot
attain to the authoritative, intrinsic evaluations it proposes to
give us.

The next kind of theory, the individualistic sort represented
by Croce, is in fact the only kind of evaluation whose criteria are
truly intrinsic. It asks simply, what is this work trying to
achieve, and has it achieved it? Frequently, one hears the objection that such hypothetical evaluation is a delusion because we
can never really know what a work was trying to achieve, only

what it in fact did. This objection is invalid. It may be true that we are never certain what a work is trying to achieve, but our guess about its aim can be correct, and with enough evidence we can approach certainty. If absolute certainty were required in literary study, not a single interpretive statement in all existing exegeses could meet the requirement. The Crocean mode of evaluation is, in fact, very widely and successfully practiced. My criticism just now of broad-genre theories is an example of it. My objection was that these theories were trying to be intrinsic and were not succeeding, and I would think that any such Crocean judgment must be considered valid. The Crocean method of formulating criteria is, then, intrinsic. But do its criteria thereby gain privileged status? I think not, for here the so-called intentional fallacy achieves its limited applicability. What difference does it make how well an aim is achieved if it is not a valuable aim? Not even Croce, I think, would judge a work good which perfectly achieved some perverse or idiotic aim. So I conclude that although Croce's theory is the only one capable of providing truly intrinsic criteria, this theoretical purity is almost entirely irrelevant to serious criticism. If common sense tells us that many intrinsic failures are more valuable in our literature than many intrinsic successes, then intrinsic success is not going to be the privileged standard we have been seeking.

It was precisely this Crocean atomism which the Chicagoans, following Aristotle, sought to overcome when they formulated the genre theory of evaluation. In Aristotle's view, it did not matter at all that Euripides might have *wanted* to compose a plot requiring stage artifice and did this admirably, for in the genre tragedy, the best kind of plot resembles the one in *Oedipus Rex* which is more conducive to the proper pleasure of tragedy. Thus, the standard is not what the work was actually aiming at, but what it should have been aiming at, whether it knew it or not. This solves the Crocean problem by positing generic criteria which exclude silly or perverted aims. At the same time, it overcomes the insuperable problem of broad-genre theories by positing criteria specifically appropriate to the work at hand. A comic novel must not have a hero whose moral flaws are so egregious as to foreclose entirely the reader's sympathy and thus his ability to laugh. To achieve comedy, the work must obey the psychological demands essential to comedy. Thus, if an author were foolish enough to attempt a comedy having a hero who is morally repugnant, the result would be disgust, not laughter, and the author would fail in his aim. In this way it is possible to deduce generic criteria which are not dependent upon the aims which a misguided or unenlightened author might actually have intended; yet such criteria would nevertheless be intrinsic to his work since they would govern the genre which subsumes the work.

It is a very neat trick, and I believe that this middle course between the Scylla of the Croceans and the Charybdis of the Coleridgeans represents the most considerable attempt yet made to solve the problem of intrinsic and thus presumably privileged evaluation. Moreover, the conceptions of the modern Aristotelians are uniquely well suited to explain an almost universal pattern of judgment in human affairs: "Yes, I see that it's well done, but I don't like that sort of thing." Or: "Yes, it's well done, but that sort of thing isn't good for people." Concepts like "that kind of thing" do very often govern our judgment whether the thing is "well done." That such judgments have shown themselves to be indispensable must be granted to Aristotle and his heirs. But for all their theoretical subtlety, the modern Aristotelians have not sponsored very much significant evaluative criticism, partly because the theory itself is defective. For in brute fact, the modern Aristotelians have attempted an impossibility. They cannot legitimately argue that the intrinsic aims of a work are different in any respect from its actual aims as intended by its author. If a writer tries to achieve laughter with a morally repugnant hero, he may not succeed (I am not sure that he could not succeed), but his failure would not lie in his refusal to conform to the ineluctable criteria of a subsumptive genre called comedy. His failure would lie in his having incompatible aims, or in having insufficient abilities to make them compatible. On this point Croce has the best of the argument:

> We must leave writers and speakers free to define the sublime or the comic, the tragic or the humorous, on every occasion as they please and as may suit the end they have in view. . . . If such definitions be taken too seriously, there happens to them what Jean Paul Richter said of all the definitions of the comic: namely, that their sole merit is *to be themselves comic* and to produce in reality the fact which they vainly try to fix logically. And who will ever logically determine the dividing line between the comic and the non-comic, between laughter and smiles, between smiling and gravity, or cut the ever varying continuum into which life melts into clearly divided parts?[9]

If an actual aim of a comedy or any other kind of work does not correspond to the generic model posited for it, then the mere model cannot impose the aim; and if the aim of the work does correspond, then the model is not needed to sanction or disclose it. The Chicago theorists, when they enter the region of immediate practice, have shown how difficult it is to be an orthodox Aristotelian in a world that is in fact Crocean. Aristotle was wrong to suppose that human productions can be classified in a definitive way like biological species, or that works of art could have intrinsic goals different from those actually aimed at by their human authors.

The supreme irony is that Aristotle is himself the source for a refutation of all these generic schemes of evaluation. The broad genre theories like those of Coleridge and the New Critics, as well as the narrow genre theories of the Chicagoans, must assume the essential similarity of the members within the genre. For the Coleridgeans, all of literature is assumed to be unified by certain distinguishing traits, just as for the Chicagoans certain species of comic novels are similarly unified. In other words, they assume that literature as a whole or some sub-genre of it has a definable essence or telos which can govern the formulation of criteria. But we may be permitted to be skeptical so long as that essence is not satisfactorily defined. According to Aristotle, the essence of any class is that system of characteristics which are shared by all its members, and which are not shared by things outside the class. Thus, a true class requires a set of distinguishing features which are inclusive within the class and exclusive outside it; it requires a differentia specifica. That, according to Aristotle, is the key to definition and to essence. But, in fact, nobody has ever so defined literature or any important genre within it. As Croce put the case: "If an empirical definition of universal validity be demanded, we can but submit this one: The sublime (or comic, tragic, humorous, etc.) is *everything* that is or shall be so *called* by those who have employed or shall employ these *words.*"[10] Croce's nominalism would hold *a fortiori* for such words as "literary" or "literature," and his view is powerfully supported in the work of Wittgenstein.[11]

So much, then, for the intrinsic evaluation of literature and its three basic strategies. Useful and even indispensable as they are, they cannot attain to the privileged status which they implicitly claim. When they are intrinsic (i.e., Crocean) they do not usually proffer significant evaluations; when they do, they are not usually intrinsic. We are left, then, with extrinsic evaluation, that is, with criteria of judgment which are not grounded in the nature of literature. We are left with the mode of Plato, Tolstoy, and, in large part, of Sidney, Johnson, Shelley, Arnold, in fact with most of the criticism that is worth terming evaluation at all. For instance, the Coleridgean mode of criticism practiced by the New Critics is, for the most part, extrinsic, despite its pretense of being otherwise; criteria like complexity, maturity, richness, compression, tension, and so forth, are (except when they happen to coincide precisely with the author's intention) extrinsic criteria. Their sanction comes entirely from the religious, moral, and aesthetic standpoint which sponsors such criteria as estimable values.[12] They are not sanctioned by anything intrinsic to the nature of literature.

Yet that is precisely the reason these extrinsic criteria have been productive of significant criticism. They induce judgments of value which transcend the aims of individual works and thereby permit comparative evaluations which have reference to larger dimensions of life. It was only when the New Critics tried to exclude certain judgments as being "extrinsic" or "unliterary" that they went astray and unnecessarily inhibited the practice of criticism. For as soon as the adjective "literary" is given accurate content in a particular usage, it turns out that the New Critics have been as unliterary as Plato or Tolstoy. In their delusion has lain their strength. Similarly, the significant criticism of the Chicago school has been extrinsic criticism. Its most important critical effort, Booth's *The Rhetoric of Fiction*, is an excellent piece of moral-aesthetic extrinsic evaluation mixed with intrinsic evaluation. That it claims to be largely Aristotelian and intrinsic in no way diminishes its importance as a persuasive and important work in the tradition of Plato.

Most evaluation worthy of the name is, then, largely extrinsic. And the criticism which has been most widely useful and esteemed has combined two kinds of extrinsic standards; it has adduced extrinsic criteria of technical excellence (as in Aristotle), and it has adduced extrinsic criteria concerning the benefit of literature to mankind (as in Plato). Even Aristotle argued platonically that good tragedy purges the audience of emotions which are deleterious to their happiness and to the good of the state. And even Plato, in *The Laws* and elsewhere, recognized that works of art can be well made or ill made, whether or not they are good for the state. But neither the Platonic nor Aristotelian kind of criterion, individually, or as is usual, complexly mixed together, can be deduced from the nature of literature. Both kinds of criterion are grounded in value-preferences which must make their own way in the world.

And in the modern world no single hierarchy of values is privileged. We lack the institutionalized authority or the genuinely widespread cultural consensus which could sponsor truly preferential criteria in literary criticism. Absolute evaluation requires an absolute; it requires a universal church. But the actual world of literary evaluation has been for some time now a protestant world where preferential criteria are in fact only the preferences of a sect. To hope for more absolute sanction is to pursue a will-o'-the-wisp.

Consciousness of this cultural fact can lead to a liberating clarity rather than to pure skepticism. The fact that no system of evaluative criteria can manage to sustain a claim to privilege does not imply that some system of values does not in reality deserve to sustain such a claim. Plato, for instance, could be right that the good of the state is the ultimate value to which all others are subordinated, and he might even be right in his conception of the good of the state. He might also be wrong. Mere men cannot pass that ultimate judgment with absolute certainty. Yet men are obliged to take a stand, and it is well to recognize that any pretense to "purely literary" literary criticism is simply to disguise one's stand even for oneself. But, if there is no privilege in literary evaluation, there is nevertheless objectivity and accuracy, and these reside entirely in the judged relationship between literature and the criteria we choose to apply to it. If our criterion is "maturity," and if we make clear what that criterion means, then our judgment of a work's maturity can be just as valid and absolute as a judgment drawn on the basis of some criterion for which we falsely claim a privileged status. The critic's choice of criteria depends upon the purposes he has in view and ultimately upon his own protestant inward light. But his evaluations upon those criteria can be absolutely accurate.

Thus, there is no valid reason to preserve any affection for the empty shibboleth "literature as literature." Its success in the world has been a measure only of its delusiveness, of its logical meaninglessness. No strategy of thought can ultimately protect the critic or the teacher from his responsibility to draw judgments about the value of literature within any context where it has for him significant value. And beyond this, the critic has a responsibility to knowledge itself: an obligation to know just what his criteria are, to know what he is doing and why.[13]

# 8
# Some Aims of Criticism

## I. The Literary Study of Literature

The dominant movement in literary criticism since the 1940s is probably best called "intrinsic criticism." In discoursing upon it, I shall occasionally use the more familiar term "New Criticism," but only on the understanding that the reference is to an international movement of very broad scope, and not to Anglo-American manifestations alone. The guiding principle of the movement, which arose in academic circles in the 1920s and 1930s, was not formalism, or close analysis, or stylistics, but rather the programmatic idea that literature should be described and estimated in its own intrinsic categories. Many present-day reactions against formalism do not really attack this central conception, but propose the substitution or addition of broader intrinsic categories like recurrent myths, period styles, genre-traits, and modes, which define other aspects of the world of literature. The original and powerful programmatic idea—that literature should be dealt with as literature and not some other thing—still remains the dominant though not the only guiding principle for the teaching and criticism of literature.

The underlying unity and broad influence of the movement can be seen in the continuing force of its insistence on literary categories. One of the objections it brought against older forms of literary study was that literature lost its essential character when viewed as a mere effect of historical influences. Literary works, it was insisted, are not mere historical documents. Their historical dimension can be understood properly only when historical forces are described in literary categories—particularly those pertaining to the traditions of literary art. The same principle—translation into literary categories—must be applied to all

124

the other dimensions of literature, moral, political, psychological, and social, in order to achieve appropriate results.

An account of the psychological dimension of literature that won few adherents but was nevertheless highly characteristic of the new program is found in a stimulating early work of I. A. Richards, *Principles of Literary Criticism* (1924). Psychologically, the most beneficial literature, in Richards's view, is the kind that harmonizes a large number of disparate and conflicting psychic impulses. Thus, a formal or purely literary criterion of excellence, similar to the kind proposed by Coleridge, is altogether concordant with Richards's psychological criterion. Literature that is formally rich and complex, and brings into unity a great many opposite and discordant elements achieves excellence both as literature and as therapy.[1] Since the two kinds of criteria coincide, the psychological values of literature can be accommodated to literary categories.

This pattern of accommodation is very widespread and is particularly interesting in its application to the moral dimension of literature. Writers like F. R. Leavis and Yvor Winters, though different in their preferences, were alike in correlating the qualities of an author's moral vision with the qualities of his style. Excellence of moral vision does not guarantee literary excellence, but the reverse does hold: literary excellence implies and requires moral wisdom, while inadequate moral conceptions will exclude an author from the highest achievements of literary art.[2] While these critics are essentially moralists of literature, they feel required to transform moral into literary judgments, thereby treating literature as literature.

In the work of W. K. Wimsatt, the principle is developed more subtly and cogently. Artistic complexity implies and reflects the moral complexity of actual life. Good literature, which is, for Wimsatt as for Richards, complex literature, will tend on the whole to have a positive moral tendency—even an immoral play like *Antony and Cleopatra*. By a structural correspondence, the moral issue can be accommodated to literary categories.[3] And Wayne Booth, proclaiming his loyalty to the principles of Chicago that Wimsatt deplored,[4] follows a very similar pattern of accommodation. If an author does not implicitly take an ethical stance, and if that stance is not one we can respect, then his devices will not effectively work upon us. His work must be judged unsuccessful under purely literary canons.[5]

The intrinsic movement is sometimes attacked for not attending to the external implications of literature, and recently Frederick Crews has condemned the criticism of Northrop Frye for this sin of omission.[6] I think it was sound of Crews to argue that Frye's work is not a departure from but belongs to the very center of intrinsic criticism. But to the complaint that he has ignored society Frye has replied with some justice that he has had in view scarcely anything else.[7] Under Frye's conception, the informing myths of literature are not just recurrent structures of poetry, drama, and fiction, but also universal constructs of the human imagination, and thus constitutive not only of literature but of society as well. For Frye (as for Shelley, whom no one would accuse of not attending to society) both social institutions and literary works are built in the smithy of the human imagination. The internal characteristics of literature reflect social and ethical implications through a system of genetically based correspondences, so that to describe the one is to describe the other. The social is *aufgehoben* in the literary.[8] The structure of this accommodation is very similar to that of Richards, Leavis, Winters, Wimsatt, and Booth.

This characteristic strategy of New Criticism can be seen as an attempt to overcome the traditional disjunction between the artistic qualities of literature (*dulce*) and its instrumental effects (*utile*). The attempt is best understood not as disinterested speculation but as part of the general program to understand literature from within. Frye hoped to make criticism a science, and for him, as for earlier theorists of New Criticism, this meant the development of categories and classifications peculiarly appropriate to the subject.[9] Such an aim would explain the common assertion of a preestablished harmony between the external effects of literature and its internal traits, allowing the former to be accommodated to the latter. For if the psychological, moral, or social effects of literature, important though they may be, are described in alien psychological, moral, or social categories, and judged according to the alien criteria of those fields, then literature becomes a mere instrument, just as for history it had been a mere document.

Even if the accommodation of external effects to literary categories should be judged logically inadmissible, the main thrust of New Criticism would be scarcely affected, for the focus of the movement has not been on the external effects of literature. Indeed, New Criticism can reasonably argue that these effects vary so greatly from one context to another that the whole unmanageable question is better left alone. While I would by no means accept such an a priori dismissal of this important subject, I do think we must concede that the intrinsic criticism of literature has been and still remains our most powerful programmatic idea.

For many years now, the very power of the idea, and its persistence, have generated protests against what has seemed an overly hermetic conception of literary criticism.[10] Academic critics have been asked to show more concern for historical and biographical contexts, for the social relevance of literature, and for our present cultural and psychological needs. Individual critics have followed these injunctions, some of them long before the pleas were made, and many teachers of literature, including some figures of importance in New Criticism, have been sympathetic to the pleas and protests. But the calls have not been answered on a big scale because so far they have not been followed by counterproposals that can compete with New Criticism in intellectual stature or practical effectiveness.

On a practical level, for example, these counterproposals do not imply educational goals sufficiently definite to form the basis of textbooks and teaching guides like *Understanding Poetry* and its counterparts in Britain and Europe. That is at the least a failure in strategy, for under our present institutions, the main consumers of literary criticism are students fulfilling course requirements and teachers setting them. It cannot be expected that some new theory of criticism will take hold if it does not reach beyond scholarly and journalistic writing to embrace the concrete goals of classroom teaching. It is permanently to the credit of New Criticism that it transformed and improved the teaching of literature. A new theoretical proposal that does not promise similarly to invigorate teaching will fail to interest those who will alone determine the success or failure of any fresh critical movement.

But the practical success of New Criticism was not based merely upon its power to generate teaching guides and classroom methods. Teachers would not have embraced its methods if they had not found in the intellectual claims of New Criticism an appeal quite separate from that of its pedagogical usefulness. Intrinsic criticism claimed to be an intellectual and theoretical advance over older forms of historical, biographical, and philological study, and that claim was accepted. The New Criticism thereby had a purely intellectual success greater than anything to be hoped for by those who attack it on the grounds that it has grown boring and can no longer meet the ideological and psychological requirements of the young. Those are not trivial objections, and they will certainly prove fatal in the end to the dominance of intrinsic criticism. Nevertheless, they are not in themselves theoretical objections which give promise of an intellectual advance.

Admittedly, the power of boredom over intellectual fashions must never be underestimated, but its positive, generative capacities are not great. When the spokesmen for New Criticism pressed their case against Old Philology, they did not claim preferment merely as agents of a new *Zeitgeist* arrived on the scene when the old and stale ideas had completed their historical mission. Their argument was of quite a different sort. In essence it said that the Old Philology had been misguided from the start; that its naive methods and aims were quite inappropriate to its subject matter; and that the whole discipline of literary study should be put on a new and permanently valid footing, with methods, aims, and assumptions truly appropriate to literature. This claim of inherent theoretical superiority was valid on many counts, and in the end, the methodological and theoretical superiority of New Criticism must be considered the main reason for its practical success inside the classroom and beyond.

Yet the current disaffections have more than temporary implications. They indicate, I believe, a flaw in the central, universally shared principle of intrinsic criticism, or at least in the assumptions on which the principle has been applied. Although the primary reason for the success of New Criticism has been its superiority to the methods it replaced, there is still room to doubt its claim of unique superiority as based on its specially appropriate and intrinsic character. The "literary study of literature" has a privileged ring to it, like "the proper study of mankind is man."[11] But what lies behind tautological formulations like the injunction to consider a poem as a poem? This methodological banner cry has not been extended to other fields—to the study of history as history, or the study of medicine as medicine. This does not mean that for literary study the formulation was meretricious or meaningless; one can only object that the meaning has not been made explicit. The Popean injunction to study literature as literature lends the program an apparently privileged status, but what the formulation in fact proposed was the study of literature as art.

This implication of the program was hardly covert. Nobody made a secret of it. Most of the major theoretical expositions (by Walzel, Richards, Crane, Wellek, Wimsatt, Staiger, Frye, and others) explicitly defined literature as art or accepted the definition as an assumption too obvious to belabor. It is difficult to remember whether Ingarden's book of 1931 was called *Das literarische Kunstwerk* and Kayser's of 1948 *Das sprachliche Kunstwerk*, or vice versa. It hardly matters, since either would serve as the title for a German version of several works originally composed in English. Even theorists who focused their attention on subjects broader than the individual literary work of art assumed, as their guiding principle, that the proper study of the critic is literature-as-art.

Is this a valid assumption? Is the study of literature as art uniquely appropriate to its subject matter, and therefore, by inherent right, the proper governing principle of criticism? In my own mind, that is the big question, and I shall try to deal with it in what follows, but first it must be said that the implicit claim of privilege by New Criticism is unquestionably justified on one point. If one goal of inquiry is to discover and define the artistic traits and values of literature, then the study of literature as art is privileged for that inquiry. It must be said further that the pursuit of this inquiry with energy and intelligence over the past four decades has advanced our understanding of literature as art beyond anything accomplished along those lines in previous times. The rhetorical analyses of Antiquity, of the Middle Ages, and the Renaissance—periods when rhetoric stood at the center of education as it no longer does—seem to me mechanical and uninformative when set alongside the best works of New Criticism. And, on the theoretical side, poetics has been advanced beyond anything achieved by Aristotle or anyone else. It is unlikely that so much would have been accomplished if New Criticism had not conceived its mission to be uniquely privileged. Whether or not that conception is valid, the accomplishments remain.

## II. The Idea of Literature

The axiom that literature-as-literature equals literature-as-art implies that the distinctive and essential feature of literature, marking it off from other forms of written speech, is its artistic character. Although this essentialistic doctrine is rarely stated in blunt nakedness, it is a necessary assumption of intrinsic criticism, and is the main implication to be drawn from phrases like "the literary work of art," "literature as literature," "poem as poem." When these implications are formulated explicitly, they run like this: Literary criticism should conform to the essential nature of its subject. The essence of literature is art. It follows that aesthetic inquiry is essentialistic and thus privileged.

Tolstoy, playing the role of the little boy who gazed on the naked emperor, would ask, "What is art? Does art have an essence?" The learned despisers of aesthetics like Tolstoy are not

only if we think aesthetics
    is the proper study of art.
I don't think that's fair: all those
    statements mean is that some attention

always fair-minded in their dismissals, and in any case the question "What is literature-as-art?" may not depend for its answer on exercises in general aesthetics. When Tolstoy objected that most works on aesthetics paid no attention to the question "What is Art?" but expended their energy on the fruitless question "What is Beauty?" the objection was unfair.[12] The very concept of art in Tolstoy's sense, which is the dominant modern sense, did not have broad currency before the last half of the nineteenth century. Some of the theorists Tolstoy chastises would not have clearly understood his question. It is probably best to set general aesthetics aside, and approach the issue in a restricted way by asking more narrowly whether literature has an artistic essence that can sanction a privileged form of criticism.

In some modern theoretical discussions this problem is avoided by focusing attention on poetry and the poem—the traditional subjects of poetics. But the principles set forth in such theories are meant to apply with various degrees of adequacy to other forms of literary art, such as novels. Similarly, other specialized theories of particular genres can bypass the question "What is literature?" by limiting the reference to those genres alone. Nevertheless, the big question about literature is always implicit in these theoretical exercises because the artistic character of poems and the other genres remains always at the center. Moreover, the subsumption of these diverse genres under literature is the unquestioned basis of the institutionalized discipline to which these discussions contribute. Certain nonliterary genres are excluded; as yet, no professor of literature has busied himself with a theoretical discussion of statutory codes.[13] The notion that there is a valid category, literature, distinct from other kinds of writing which do not qualify, is a ubiquitous and, in many respects, as I wish to concede from the start, valid idea.

The idea is, however, surprisingly recent in its correlation with a single word. Although "literature" occurs very early in English, it did not normally refer even to a corpus of works before the nineteenth century. The only meaning given in any edition of Johnson's *Dictionary* is: that which a person has read, his literature, his learning.[14] I find no example of the word in its present, aesthetic connotation before the 1850s. When De Quincey contrasted the literature of knowledge and the literature of power, he was moving in his second category toward the current meaning, but the category of literature per se was still quite undifferentiated.[15] Nor can I find the modern usage in Hazlitt or in Coleridge, whose *Biographia Literaria* is a history of his reading, thinking, and writing that gives as much weight to philosophers as to poets, and to his own journalistic and philosophical work as to his poetry. Coleridge conveys the modern sense of "literature" by the phrase "polite letters," sometimes by "poetry."[16] Similarly, when Hazlitt writes of "American Literature," the essay which uses that phrase in its title focuses on the sermons and moral tracts of Dr. Channing.[17]

The French, apparently, began to restrict the sense of the word before the English or Americans. Some uncertain examples of such restriction for *littérature* can be found in the late eighteenth century, particularly in Voltaire, who wished to exclude merely technical manuals from the honorific classification.[18] Diderot and his colleagues, besides urging the study of ancient authors under "Littérature," correlate the term with "les Sciences proprement dites."[19] Thus before the nineteenth century in France, *littérature* had by no means captured the semantic field of *belles lettres*, though the English use of "literature" late in the nineteenth century was probably, as with many words of aesthetic orientation, an adoption from a more precocious French usage.

In itself, this kind of historical semantics has little significance for the theoretical question I have posed, and no great reliance can be placed even on the precision of the historical inferences themselves, which need the support of more detailed researches. Nevertheless, some pertinent inferences can be drawn. We can surmise, for instance, that although an idea corresponding to the modern sense of "literature" may have existed before the later nineteenth century, indeed certainly did exist under formulations like "polite letters," the unitary force of the conception was not very central or even very natural to earlier cultures. Strong evidence, including that accumulated in controlled experiments, exists to support the view that unitary words tend to replace phrases only when a new interest or importance is attached to the concept represented by the phrase.[20] The implication is that sometime in the later nineteenth century, but not before, phrases like "polite letters" no longer suited the new importance and prominence of the unitary conception that still attaches to the word "literature."

Why did the unity of the conception appear so tardily to the minds of men? Probably for the reasons which delayed the modern sense of "art," and which hindered the emergence of "science" in its current acceptation. I believe it is reasonable to guess that in English the modern senses of "literature," "science," and "art" are all inventions of the Victorians. Certainly, they were the first to require these interrelated conceptions, while the props of revealed religion grew ever weaker as foundations for their spiritual world. "Art" and "literature" are secularized conceptions which embrace writers of the most divergent religious and ethical persuasions within a unified humanistic orientation. That is a plausible inference to be drawn from the preoccupations and linguistic traits of a writer like Matthew Arnold, who as Wellek points out, is also one of those to whom we owe the exaltation of the word "criticism," along with the word "culture."[21]

*Or because of the success of science.*

The rather late origins of the unitary sense of "literature" do not impair the validity of the concept. What the relative modernity of the word helps explain is why no definition of "literature" can embrace the current meaning through a grouping of traditional genres. A definition adequate to the modern meaning seems to require the modern category of "art." For instance, the following might be thought to cover the dominant present usage: "Literature comprises any linguistic work, written or oral, which has significant aesthetic qualities." Our modern usage can no longer be restricted as to genre, nor can it be limited to works having significant aesthetic intentions, since many works belonging to literature did not intend a predominantly aesthetic appeal. That is readily seen in a book like Moulton's *The Bible as*

*Why? surely there has been discussion of this: is one to deny it.*

*but may have it*

*Literature*, or in standard courses that begin with the Bible (as literature), move on to Homer and Greek tragedy, through Shakespeare and Dickens to T. S. Eliot.[22] Nobody misunderstands the title of Moulton's book, and few protest the formulation of immensely heterogeneous syllabi for literary courses. The only definition adequate to our sense of literature is one that avoids terms implying common independent traits. Our definition must therefore be further amended: "Literature comprises any linguistic work, written or oral, which has significant aesthetic qualities *when described in aesthetic categories.*" The further qualification is required to bring otherwise subordinate aesthetic qualities to the center of attention. The modern concept of literature implies a modern, aesthetic mode of perception. Literature cannot be defined adequately without taking that mode of perception into account.

If that is indeed the only kind of definition adequate to our present usage of "literature," then the question about the privileged nature of aesthetic criticism appears in a new light. Because an aesthetic approach inheres in the very concept of literature, it appears to be indeed intrinsic. The difficulty is that the concept of literature is not itself a privileged category for the works it embraces. Since literary works were not always conceived under a predominantly aesthetic mode, we cannot assume that a stress on aesthetic categories corresponds to the essential nature of individual literary works. Other categories, including instrumental, ethical, and religious ones, may be more correspondent to their individual emphases and intentions. An intrinsic critic might reply, "Yes, that is all very well, but we want to know these works *as literature.*" To which no objection can be raised except to observe that such a pursuit is not necessarily intrinsic, and that whether the inquiry is specially appropriate to the nature of a work depends, ad hoc, on the individual case. We can accept the classification "literature" as valid, but not as privileged, and it follows that we must say exactly the same for the literary study of literature. It is valid, but not privileged.

I have argued elsewhere the general point that no critical

approach to a wide multiplicity of works can possibly be privileged or intrinsic.[23] The only activity attendant upon criticism that has a privileged character is the construction of meaning, which is no necessary part of criticism. One must, of course, understand a linguistic work in some degree before discussing it, but one's understanding need not be the main subject of one's criticism. And even understanding (i.e. the construction of original meaning) as contrasted with misunderstanding has only an ethical and not an ontological claim to privilege. It is well known that criticism based on misunderstanding can be valuable and even valid in some respects. The most one can say for aesthetic criticism is that it is intrinsic to the concept of literature, which is not itself an intrinsic concept. Aesthetic criticism must therefore relinquish its principal claim.

We should go further. In one respect aesthetic criticism has been distortive. By claiming to be intrinsic to the nature of literature, it implies that the nature of literature is aesthetic. But, in fact, literature has no independent essence, aesthetic or otherwise. It is an arbitrary classification of linguistic works which do not exhibit common distinctive traits, and which cannot be defined as an Aristotelian species. Aesthetic categories are intrinsic to aesthetic *inquiries,* but not to the nature of literary works. Exactly the same can be said of ethical and psychological categories, or any critical categories whatever. They are intrinsic only to the inquiries for which they are appropriate. The idea of literature is not an essentialistic idea, and no critical approach can, without distortion, make essentialistic claims upon literature. The methods and aims of criticism must be justified on other grounds.

## III. The Aims of Criticism

Those aims are ultimately general and abstract, but it is pertinent to look first at a practical side of our present situation. I ventured the sociological prediction that no critical program will succeed in the present day unless it generates practical aims and

*[handwritten marginalia: This needs to be demonstrated here, or at least proposes views given here]*

*[handwritten marginalia at bottom: That there is such a thing as the class, "literature"]*

procedures that apply to the classroom. This may seem doubtful in view of the current instinct of students to believe that more truth and value are found in underground studies than in those pursued within institutions. But the teacher's instinct of self-preservation has gradually made the content of established courses resemble ever more closely whatever can be discovered underground. Literary study is at present astonishingly hetero-geneous. In some American universities little remains that the underground can call its own. I am not referring just to courses that stress or include pornography, but to the whole range of subject matters and their mixtures, historical-modal, generic-thematical, modal-generical, historic-thematical, covering, for instance, "The Literature of Fantasy," "Women in Literature," "The Black Man in Literature," "Patristic Elements in Anglo-Saxon Literature." The aesthetic mode of perception can no longer be considered the governing mode, and the only vestige that remains of its former potency is the continued cheerful use of the word "literature" in the titles of these courses. This may be a mere concession to academic propriety, without further signi-ficance, and probably no critical program could bring concep-tual order to this multeity, which has far outstripped all current descriptions of modern literary criticism. Perhaps conceptual order should not be the aim. But the present realities can hardly be ignored. In contemplating the function of criticism at the present time, necessity as well as duty direct the mind to the aims of literary education.

The current pedagogical expansion of literature suggests we may be gradually returning to a more venerable, undifferen-tiated usage under which "literature" covers everything worth preserving in written form, whether or not it has artistic merit. If so, the process is entirely natural. The domain of literature was quite heterogeneous even under the aesthetic dispensation, and when that approach began to seem one-sided, it was natural to extend the capacious domain by including works of value that have little aesthetic appeal. The best that is thought and said is not always said well, even if it ought to be, and the aims of humanistic education do not necessarily coincide with traditional academic boundary lines. Humane studies have a natural tendency to be imperialistic. The study of history has constantly encroached upon literary and philosophical subjects, especially in the vigorous fields of intellectual and cultural history. To the extent that philosophy has kept within narrow confines in recent years, it has withered as a vigorous subject of instruction in the humanities. On the other hand, and quite regardless of interdepartmental courtesies, even the most imperialistic subject needs a center. It needs predominant emphases determined by its educational missions, and these need to be defined in some relation to other humane studies. We need to know where we fit in, and what we ought specially to do.

The academic success of New Criticism was enhanced because it seemed to supply a center for literary study. Just as its intrinsic claims argued its centrality, so did its battle cry "autonomy" support the natural, centripetal impulse of the discipline. Autonomy was asserted for the literary subject matter and for literary methods. The discipline thereby defined itself over against other disciplines, and was able to defend its territorial rights and independence.[24] This center has proved to be unstable, not just through the natural imperialism of humanistic subjects, which resists the centripetal impulse, but also through the inadequacy of "autonomy" and its corollaries for defining the special missions of literary education. The literary work of art can be sealed off for contemplation, or confined to the "world of literature," but it is a philosophical mistake to argue that this procedure is sanctioned by the special ontological status of literature, or that the methods of literary study are different in principle from other kinds of inquiry. This philosophical difficulty shows itself on a practical level in the contortions that are required when you attempt to accommodate all the important traits and values of literature within purely literary categories.

The difficulty is venerable and undoubtedly permanent. The central example in the history of criticism has been the unresolved tension, going back to Plato at least, between technical and instrumental excellence in poetry. Aristotle's implication that good tragedy, being purgative, is good for the state, is not a sufficient answer (whether or not it was so intended) to the more general problem Plato raised. A work can be technically (artistically) good, yet have bad, indifferent, or good effects. A work can be technically bad, yet have good, indifferent, or bad effects. What teaches may not please; what pleases may not instruct.[25] The pansynergist Coleridge gave priority to pleasure over instruction in the domain of poetry, which, he said, teaches *through* pleasure, but not even Coleridge claimed instructiveness for all poetry that pleases. In recent days the old tension has manifested itself as the literary excellence of literature versus its relevance.

This tension has never been successfully resolved in the realm of theory, though many impressive attempts have been recorded. And yet, it is another fact in the history of criticism that technical and instrumental judgments are woven both together in the work of the most honored and durable practical critics. The best critics have not been categorical purists. If you judge under instrumental categories, according to the probable effects of literature, you will judge like Plato. If you restrict yourself cogently and rigorously to aesthetic categories, you will theorize like de Gourmont. If you judge literature as art, your criticism will benefit if somewhere along the line you make a logical or categorical mistake. Only the critic who uses both categories and embraces both kinds of value does justice to the aims of literary education, and by extension, the aims of criticism. Intrinsic theory has encouraged the belief that aesthetic categories can implicitly embrace instrumental values, a mistake which has led to a one-sided emphasis on the technical aspects of literature and a neglect of straightforward ethical judgments. What we need is not a theoretical synthesis, which is impossible, but a restoration of balance in theory as well as practice.

But the road of excess leads to counterexcesses. Instead of a restoration of balance we could be in for a moralistic, not to say self-righteous, rebellion against aestheticism that would be less serviceable to humane education than the one-sided aestheticism it replaced. The technical, aesthetic kind of literary study at least opens up a world not explored in other humane subjects, whereas the ideological touchstones that are now applied to literature (racism, male chauvinism, etc.) are also applied without restriction to history, social studies, and some of the natural sciences. Within this universal revisionism, literary study has no special contribution to make. A dizzy oscillation from extreme Aristotelianism to extreme Platonism is not a restoration of balance.

As the patron saint of literary education, my candidate is Matthew Arnold, whose contraries Sweetness and Light seem especially appropriate for describing the recurrent tensions of literary criticism. Arnold saw that neither the aesthetic nor the moralistic attitude to life and literature can be reduced to its contrary. He also perceived that the function of criticism is determined by the needs of the present time, not by some eternal formulation. Yet he was not an historical relativist. The aims of criticism change with history only because the deeper principle of balance is absolute and therefore requires different applications at different times. This absolute principle of balance is the antique norm of human fulfillment—the classical ideal of harmony under which all the conflicting appetences of life are nourished, with none subjected to the tyrannical domination of another. Thus, for Arnold, neither an aesthetic nor an instrumental conception of literature can alone suffice. Pursued with provincial excess, both kinds of criticism restrict the range of values in literature, and betray the heterogeneity of its nature and our own.

This classical ideal of balance, governing culture, education, and criticism, is at bottom an ethical ideal; indeed, it is the ground principle of the *Nicomachean Ethics*. In my opinion Arnold is profoundly right to set the aims of criticism on foundations that can be described ultimately in ethical terms. Indeed, the chief justification for aesthetic contemplation and a moral holiday is ultimately an ethical justification. The foundation of literary criticism, including the scholarly and scientific study of literature, cannot be the special nature of the subject matter, since literature has no special nature. The foundation for the aims of criticism is the answer given to the ethical question "What are

*not to illuminate
the thing itself
because it's worth it*

the special contributions that criticism and literary education
can make at the present time?"

We need to keep our *special* obligations in view, for the
general goals of fullness and balance hold for all humanistic
culture, just as the admonition to know the best that is thought
and said transcends any single field of learning. Our special
contribution is not restricted to aesthetic concerns. We seem
now to be relinquishing our overemphasis on the artistic aspect
of literature, and I have tried to show the theoretical justification
for our doing so. That hardly means we should entirely abandon
the aesthetic approach; it means only that we should keep it in
bounds and resist its essentialistic claims. The soundest justification for aesthetic inquiries in literary education is that they
pertain to one side of human nature and should be pursued
somewhere. If departments of literature do not pursue them,
probably nobody else will.

The same defense can be offered for keeping poetry and prose
fiction as our central subject matter, along with the writings of
Kierkegaard, Eldridge Cleaver, Plato, and other sages in the
continuum of literature. Poetry and fiction are worth studying,
and if we don't keep them alive in humanistic education, nobody
else will. That is the only justification we need. We do not need
to claim a false ontological or elitist status for these writings, or
attempt any but heuristic definitions of their nature. The approach we take to them should be determined by the needs of the
time, and the needs of the inquiry we have chosen to pursue, not
by the presumptuous claims of any special method.

If we follow this argument whither it leads, we accept as being
literary not only sociological or linguistic or historical or political inquiry, we also accept a very broad conception of the
canon of literature—one closer to the conception that prevailed
before the late nineteenth century. Under that older conception,
literature comprises everything worthy to be read, preferably
the best thoughts expressed in the best manner, but above all the
best thoughts. I have said that this is a venerable conception of
literature. Let me quote an interesting statement by Johan Huizinga about the idea of literature in the Renaissance:

In its direct expression . . . the sense of rebirth applied almost exclusively to literary culture, the broad field of study and poetry covered by the term *bonae literae*. Rabelais speaks of the "restoration of *bonnes lettres*" as a generally known incontrovertible fact. . . . In 1559 Jacques Amyot wrote to Henry II in the dedication of his translation of Plutarch (which provided so much material for Montaigne and Shakespeare): "To you will be given the praise for having gloriously crowned and completed the work founded and begun by the great King Francis your late father, to cause *les bonnes lettres* to be reborn in this noble realm.". . . Erasmus is credited as the one "who well-nigh first of all cherished the rebirth of letters, *renascentes bonas litteras.*"[26]

It would be a most interesting subject of literary inquiry to discover just how the grand, broad, and noble conception of literature as *les bonnes lettres* disappeared and was replaced by the narrower, more decadent conception expressed by *les belles lettres*.

One historical fact we do know. We know how English literature first became an accepted field of study in England, late in the nineteenth century. In his tireless battle during the 1880s against the study of mere philology at Oxford, Churton Collins invited opinions from a great many important personages in Britain as to whether Oxford should institute a regular course of study in English literature as literature, rather than as documentation in the history of the language. Collins saw literary study as replacing the classics as the basis of humane education. Among the replies he received and later published in a special issue of the *Pall Mall Gazette* in 1887 is one I should like to quote. It is from Edward Dowden, the Shakespearean critic and biographer of Shelley:

While the study of literature may have something to fear on the one hand, from the science of philology, which threatens to usurp its place and name, it views with alarm, on the other hand, what I may name the *belles lettres* heresy. The study of literature—English or other—is not a study solely of what

is graceful, attractive, and pleasure-giving in books; it attempts to understand the great thoughts of the great thinkers.
To know Greek literature we must know Aristotle; to know
French literature we must know Descartes. In English literature of the eighteenth century Berkeley and Butler and Hume
are greater names than Gray and Collins.

Dowden's conception of *les bonnes lettres* is closer to that of
the Renaissance than to our own. If his view had prevailed, the
accepted canon of literature would be very much broader than it
has been in the recent past. What Dowden shared with Erasmus
and Amyot was the idea that Wisdom and Knowledge are para-
mount criteria for deciding what should be read and studied—
that in the study of letters, Wisdom and Knowledge are as
important as Imagination, and Sentiment, and Art. Nor is Dowden's view very different on this point from the view of Matthew
Arnold. Arnold pressed for striking a balance between the values of Sweetness and the values of Light, a balance in culture
between the ethical and the aesthetic. Certainly he was not in
favor of confusing the two. Although the Victorians were re-
sponsible for our modern aesthetic conception of literature,
some of them at least must be credited with firmly criticizing that
one-sided conception.

   The Victorians must also be credited with a renaissance of their
own in the domain of plain prose. Victorian prose is a standard
literary subject even under a belletristic conception of literature,
though that is not the most fruitful conception for studying, for
instance, Mill's *Essay on Liberty*. (And in the spirit of Dowden it
is tempting to add that in English literature of the nineteenth
century, Charles Darwin is a greater and a more interesting
name than Walter Pater.) One of the most important tasks of
criticism at the present time is the reintegration of plain prose,
even plainest prose, into the canon of literature. The first step
would be to regard literature as verbal discourse, not merely as
verbal artifact.

   If we now look back at the modern victory that was won over
philology, in the name of humane letters, we can see that Churton Collins's revolution was in the end betrayed by aesthetic

theories. For to be a specialist in elite verbal artifacts is to be just as narrow in a different way as to be a mere philologist. Still, I believe it is true that our teaching of literature is now on the whole broader and better than the theories that govern our current scholarship and criticism. In the 1940s it seemed important to assert our autonomy and to isolate the literary artifact from the continuum of verbal discourse. In the 1970s there seems a narrowness in such a notion that makes us wish to change those lakes to ocean. We are now willing to teach, in fact if not in theory, just about anything in print. No theory of literature currently available can account for the immense diversity of books that are actually taught in American departments of literature. In practice, at least, the prescription to understand literary works exclusively as verbal artifacts has been repudiated. Many people, no matter how they describe what they do, teach on Platonic and Arnoldian principles. Hence I do not want to end my critique of intrinsic theory with a plea that we should teach valuable books of many sorts in addition to valuable works of art. A sound instinct has already begun to effect that change despite our theories. I shall conclude with a very modest proposal.

If the general aim of literary study is to civilize and humanize, we should be more concerned with the humanization of ordinary writing and speaking. The jargon of the technocrat whose terms of "input" and "output" turn us metaphorically into machines is now part of our modern literature. For who can explain where the continuum of literature begins and ends? Certainly we can say in general that the plain style in prose is the most important style in literature because it is so widespread and contains so much of the best that is said and thought in the world, but above all because the plain style in prose is the chief vehicle of mass literacy in modern cultural life. When the plain style becomes dehumanized and grotesque, that is of greater consequence for the tenor and quality of our culture than the character of our poetry and fiction.

In the past few decades when we isolated the literary work of art from the continuum of discourse we were inclined to separate the teaching of literature from what is humbly called the teaching of composition. Under the dominance of intrinsic theory, composition courses, which could be called courses in the rhetoric of plain, humane prose, disappeared from the curriculum. Under the impression that literature exists in a domain separate from their own humbler efforts to write, our students were willing to discuss the subtlest stylistic nuances in poetry in uncommunicative and barbaric prose. Why not? Poetry is literature, while their stuff is just essay writing. But the sage theorist who told M. Jourdain he was speaking prose might tell our students that what they are writing is literature.

We have already begun to enlarge the canon of literature and so enlarge the sphere of humane letters that we teach. But that is an enlargement of passive literacy. We should also enlarge and humanize the sphere of active literacy. English professors complain of language pollution as though, like bad weather, it were something they were powerless to change. In fact, English professors teach the teachers who teach millions of pupils in the biggest single educational enterprise of our literate society. As a group, English professors could exert as much influence, if they decided to, as that handful of renaissance humanists who attempted to defeat the cultural barbarity of an age by their revival of *les bonnes lettres*. In the era of mass literacy, a transparent style is just as important in literature as a beautiful or iconic style. Of course it is more important. Bluntly, we ought to be teaching composition with as much thoughtfulness and energy as we teach great books and great works of art. Active literacy and passive literacy are not separate under the ideal of humane letters, good matter in a good manner. To foster that ideal of literature and make it live in the humblest writing and speaking could be our most significant contribution to a revival of *les bonnes lettres*.

But in the end it would be misleading to suggest that any aim of criticism or of literary study has more than a contingent claim upon us. No form of criticism is inherently privileged. If this conclusion removes some external props from our ethical decisions, the consolation is that the props have not been sturdy and reliable. Another consolation is that literature, like criticism, is more capacious and, in its untrammeled diversity, more important than any aesthetic conception of literature has made it out to be.

He doesn't address the
Question. He wants
"culture", "the best
thought & written" —
He wants morality
& civilization,
but he's not interested
in art as a special
activity or dimension
of human existence
that has a very par-
ticular role in
culture-making and
value-making.

# 9

# Afterword: Knowledge and Value

*If a man is sufficiently unimaginative to produce evidence in support of a lie, he might just as well speak the truth at once.*

—Oscar Wilde

The reader will have noticed that the two concepts which have presided over these chapters—meaning and significance—bear a close resemblance to the concepts knowledge and value. Meaning is the stable object of knowledge in interpretation, without which wider humanistic knowledge would be impossible. The chief interest of significance, on the other hand, is in the unstable realm of value. The significance of meaning in a particular context determines its value in that context. For, significance names the relationships of textual meaning, and value is a relationship, not a substance. Value is value-for-people. Textual meaning has wide interest only when it has actual or potential value for a number of people. And this value changes. A poem may have a very different value for me at age twenty and age forty. It may possess different values for people in different cultural contexts. A poem has no absolute value.

Hence, the stability of textual meaning is no sufficient anchor in the shifting currents of value. Knowledge is not unquestionably a sufficient end. If a text is going to be worthless to most people in most contexts, then a knowledge of its meaning, no matter how accurate and scholarly, is knowledge without value. Pure *scientia*, knowledge for its own sake, is a pathetic fallacy. Who is knowledge, for whose sake we know? If value is that which is valuable for people, a lot of literary knowledge is at once valid and trivial. Those who argue for academic freedom have only gained a starting point when they have won their battle.

Because humanistic inquiry is free, it requires justification, and entails all the anxieties of freedom. Free inquiry implies choice: of subjects, of emphasis, of problems. And choice cannot be ethically or axiologically neutral. To pursue one inquiry is to neglect another. Valid interpretation is not enough. Some knowledge is not worth having.

Textual commentary is threatened nowadays by a bigger danger than the innocent accumulation of worthless knowledge. In its decadently skeptical forms, it threatens to degrade knowledge and value at once, simply by attempting to create value as a substitute for knowledge. Some French theorists, Derrida and Foucault, for instance, along with their American disciples, hold to the doctrine that since genuine knowledge of an author's meaning is impossible, all textual commentary is therefore really fiction or poetry. Emancipated by this insight, we can face the *écriture* of the past without illusion, as representing no stable or accessible meaning. We can write about writing with new-found creativity and freedom, knowing that we ourselves are creating a new fiction which will itself be fictionalized by those who read us. The challenge is to make these fictions creatively, interestingly, valuably.

Skepticism in the humanities is not confined to the French or to literary theory. It goes back to the nineteenth century and wears many guises.[1] Marxists, for instance, prefer the word "ideology" to the word "fiction." Certainly, historians had composed Whig or Tory histories long before Marx wrote of "ideology" or Mannheim of "the sociology of knowledge." But the word "knowledge" cannot be taken seriously in such a phrase, any more than can the word "truth" in "the sociology of truth." I do not find any structural differences among the various relativisms which beset the humanist. The pattern of skepticism is the same whether one applies old-fashioned terms like *worldview*, *ideology*, and *the sociology of knowledge*, or up-to-date terms like *Welt*, *difference*, *episteme*, or *paradigm*. All of them say that humanistic inquiry is enclosed within a windowless framework which provides access to no other framework; humanistic inquiry is determined by ideology taken in its broadest sense.

I do not mean to suggest that only humanists subscribe to this
dogmatic relativism. It is also accepted by those scientists, few in
number, who accept Kuhn's concept of the *paradigm* as set forth
in *The Structure of Scientific Revolutions*. It is greatly significant
that Kuhn's theories have won wider acceptance among humanists than scientists. Humanists frequently apply the term *paradigm* to their own domains, despite Kuhn's recent warning
against such application.[2] They no doubt do so on the assumption that Kuhn's term represents a recent, documented, scientific
version of *worldview, ideology, episteme*, not to mention *Welt,
approach, perspective*, and *language*, the last four representing
relativistic dogmas challenged in earlier chapters of this book.

It is especially useful to perceive the structural similarity of
Kuhn's paradigm, with all the other terms which make knowledge relative to, and trapped inside some prison-house of the
mind—all these terms which stand for Kantianism gone mad. It
is useful because Kuhn's theory has been examined and found
wanting by some first-class epistemologists, while the theories
of, say, M. Foucault have not been subjected to criticism sufficiently imposing to cause him to write a concessionary "Post-
script" such as one finds in Kuhn's second edition. If Kuhn's
theory is incorrect in principle, all structurally similar theories
are incorrect in principle because the flaw lies precisely in their
structure, in their insistence on the incommensurability, the in-
communicability of paradigms, ideologies, worldviews, and so
on.

The flaw in all such dogmatic relativism is exposed by Sir Karl
Popper, in his critique of Kuhn, with a trenchancy that cannot
be improved upon: *"The Myth of the Framework is, in our time,
the central bulwark of irrationalism. My counter-thesis is that it
simply exaggerates a difficulty into an impossibility."*[3] In chapters 1 and 5 of this book, I argued that the framework-myth of
"perspective" consistently exaggerates a difficulty into an impossibility. In chapter 4 I attacked the framework-myth of language, the most sacred of all, by showing that although it may
be difficult to convey exactly the same meaning through different linguistic forms, it is not impossible to do so. Of course, it is
all too possible that paradigms, languages, and ideologies do
determine the results of inquiry. The Myth of the Framework

simply exaggerates a common occurrence into a universally nec- ᴍ/
essary one.

But ideology is far more likely to determine the results of inquiry when the inquirer assumes that it must do so. If one paradigm cannot talk to another, if different languages cannot convey identical meanings, then no attempt need be made to discover a truth common to several diverse frameworks, that is, the truth of the case. But if ideology, not truth, determines the results of inquiry, why undertake inquiry at all? It is then just a charade in the service of ideology. Why not compose Whig and Tory histories? Why not make interpretation a tour de force, an interesting charade? But if this underlying skepticism is itself quite wrong, and if it does not pave the royal road to humanistic value, perhaps the humanities contribute something more valuable than exercises founded on a skepticism embraced by both the producers and consumers of humanistic scholarship.

Literary study is at present the most skeptical and decadent branch of humanistic study, for a number of causes, among which an important one is its anxiety-ridden insistence, more emphatic than in any other field, on distinguishing itself from natural science. If poetry is the antipodes to science, then knowledge of poetry must be the antipodes to scientific knowledge; so runs the nonsequitur. Humanistic knowledge is different from the kind of knowledge sought in the "hard" sciences, or the "exact" sciences. Unlike these, the humanities are soft and inexact, virtues which bring them closer to "life." The humanities seek a knowledge that is not neutral like that of science, but infused with value. But such contrasts are, bluntly, false. Value is the motivation of inquiry in all disciplines, not the special preserve of the humanities. And exactitude of knowledge is a variable in all fields. To recognize the result of an inquiry as an inexact approximation is to achieve exactness of knowledge. Despite the Myth of the Framework, a cognitive element exists in all humanistic study. And despite the century-old distinction between humanistic and scientific inquiry, the cognitive elements in both have exactly the same character.

The attempt to formulate a satisfactory theoretical distinction between the cognitive element in the humanities and in the natural sciences has an interesting and predominantly German history. Whether the debate (conducted mainly by neo-Kantians toward the end of the nineteenth century) was influenced by the appropriate neutrality of the word *Wissenschaft* still remains an unanswered question. (The closest English equivalent to *Wissenschaft* is the word "discipline," which is not close enough.) In any case, it became convenient to conduct the debate by distinguishing the *Geisteswissenschaften* or *Kulturwissenschaften* on the one side from the *Naturwissenschaften* on the other. And the purpose of the distinction was to defend the autonomous character of knowledge in the humanities against the intellectual imperialism of natural science. For if humane knowledge tried to compete with science on its own, positivistic grounds, then the humanities would belie their native character and turn into mere pseudoscience.

In the first volume of his *Introduction to the Humane Sciences* (1883), Wilhelm Dilthey attempted to set forth coherent theoretical foundations for the *Geisteswissenschaften*, just as William Whewell had done for the natural sciences in his *History of the Inductive Sciences* (1837) and John Stuart Mill had done in his *System of Logic* (1843). Dilthey's attempt, however, was strikingly influenced by these two books, and his epistemological models were dependent upon those of natural science. The main distinctions he drew between the two great domains pertained to their subject matter rather than their methodology.

This view was sharply challenged by Wilhelm Windelband eleven years later in his famous lecture on "History and Natural Science." He proposed that the division of knowledge into natural and humane sciences was justified not merely by their different subject matters, but also and more fundamentally "by the formal character of their different epistemological goals," for "the one seeks *general* laws, while the other seeks *particular* historical facts." Natural science, therefore, is *nomothetic*, or legislative, while humane knowledge is *idiographic*, or unique and individual. Subsumption under general laws in the natural sciences is *Erklären*, but the aim of humane studies is *Verstehen*, understanding the particular in its uniqueness. Windelband's formulation took hold and it still remains the dominant conception of humanists.

The ensuing discussion comprised Dilthey's answer, *Naturwissenschaften und Geisteswissenschaften* (1895), and a book by Heinrich Rickert, *Kulturwissenschaften und Naturwissenshaften* (1899). The debate is still instructive, not for what it resolved, but for what it failed to resolve. In replying to Windelband, Dilthey was surely right to insist that generalizing and particularizing aims are common to both domains; hence Windelband was wrong. But Dilthey's counterdistinction was not more adequate or definitive—namely, the distinction between the internal and the external sciences. All the distinctions brought forward in the debate were useful as indications of preponderant tendencies in the natural sciences and the humanities, but as adequate subsumptive generalizations, they were and are total failures.

The debate about the nature of the humanities did not stop with Dilthey and Windelband, nor did the theory of science stop with Whewell and Mill, but I shall venture to suggest that at least one element of scientific theory is by now widely accepted and is identical with a widely held theory of cognitive inquiry in the humanities. The progress of knowledge and its consolidation are governed by the critical testing of hypotheses with reference to evidence and logic. If we look at any field of inquiry, we discover that it can be described as a congeries of hypotheses, some of them well accepted and others in rivalry with alternative hypotheses. We also discover a large body of evidence relevant to those hypotheses and potentially relevant to others not yet conceived. Under this conception, all inquiry is a process directed toward increasing the probability of learning the truth. This probability is, of course, increased whenever supportive evidence is increased. On the other hand, when hypotheses are called into doubt by the discovery of unfavorable evidence, then some adjustment is made, or some rival hypothesis accepted, or the whole issue is thrown into doubt. But in all these latter cases, the direction is still toward increased probability of truth, since the very instability imposed by unfavorable evidence reduces

confidence in previously accepted hypotheses and to that extent
reduces the probability of error. Knowledge in all fields thus
turns out to be a process rather than a static system, and the
direction of the process is toward increased probability of learning the truth.

Now this is a very abstract and simplified model for inquiry,
but it is the *kind* of model that every serious inquirer assumes.
Furthermore, it is an accurate model to the extent that it is
widely assumed. For I have referred not only to the logical
relationship between evidence, hypothesis, and probability, but
also to a communal enterprise that exists only to the extent that
this logical relationship remains the paradigm (or ideology!) for
the members of a community of inquirers. On the simplest level,
the members of a community cannot even maintain an increasing body of evidence unless past evidence is stored and is
brought to bear, when relevant, on hypotheses presently entertained. Nor can the model be accurate if unfavorable evidence is
suppressed by a conspiracy of the inquiring community. Nor is
the model descriptive if no one bothers to bring unfavorable
evidence to bear upon a hypothesis to which it is relevant. Thus
in a special sense, there *is* a sociology of knowledge on which
inquiry depends, on which all *scientia* depends. And to the
extent that this sense of the communal enterprise collapses, so
does the discipline itself collapse as a discipline. Hence, this
communal concept of inquiry is a stable and permanent paradigm that transcends the meaning given to paradigm in Kuhn's
*Structure of Scientific Revolutions.*

Now it is perfectly true that not all the individual members in
a discipline preserve a selfless devotion to the communal enterprise. The inspiriting description of such devotion in Max Weber's *Wissenschaft als Beruf* remains one of Weber's ideal
types. The spirit of advocacy and the spirit of vanity are almost
never completely absent in any individual endeavor. And this,
no doubt, will complicate any accurate *description* of a discipline. But healthy and progressive disciplines do exist. Somehow, even if partly through counter advocacy and counter vanity, past evidence is borne upon present hypotheses, and unfavorable evidence is sought in order to test hypotheses. A sense of

the community exists precisely because a sense of the discipline exists. The process of knowledge occurs *on the level of the discipline*. Despite individual eccentricities, brilliant guesses accompanied by brilliant perversities, the direction of knowledge goes forward at the level of the discipline. The probability of truth does in fact increase even in the humanities, so long as the sense of the inquiring community persists and inferences are drawn at the level of the discipline.

The communal aspect of knowledge insures that widespread skepticism will bring into existence the historical grounds for skepticism in a discipline. If there is a decline in commitment to the critical testing of hypotheses against all the known relevant evidence, and if the consolidation and discovery of evidence are neglected, then the process of knowledge ceases, and skepticism regarding the actuality of that process is entirely warranted. But the converse is also true. Commitment to the logic of inquiry and to the communal nature of a discipline guarantees an actual process of knowledge, and this holds for every subject of inquiry, including every subject in the humanities.

The communal conception of a discipline is widely assumed in the humanities, but also widely undercut by the humanists' emphasis on rhetoric. Obviously, the consolidated knowledge within a discipline has nothing directly to do with rhetoric. On the other hand, the communal acceptance of hypotheses has much to do with persuasion, and persuasion in doubtful matters requires attention to rhetoric. Furthermore, the goals of humanists often comprise aims that go beyond the aim of knowledge, such as taking aesthetic pleasure in discourse or persuading readers to adopt value preferences that can be related to the cognition of a subject matter. Thus the perennial questions arise: Is Clio science or muse? Is literary criticism an art or a science? The importance of rhetoric makes these appear to be difficult questions in the humanities, but in fact they are not. Obviously, rhetoric can subserve both knowledge and intellectual chicanery; rhetoric can make the worse appear the better reason. But when a discipline is viewed as a communal enterprise, the hypotheses it tests are not bound to any single expression of them.

(See chapter 4, p. 73.) Hypotheses have to be communicated as well as tested, but *what* is communicated (that is, propositions) must be used, tested, and expressed by others in a different form. If this condition is not met, the hypothesis is not really subject to criticism at the level of the discipline and has nothing to do with knowledge. It is therefore essential to distinguish hypotheses and evidence from the rhetoric used to convey them. The *writing* of history is an art, or can be, but history is not an art; it is a discipline, which is to say *scientia*. The same is true implicitly of literary studies, though one sometimes despairs that this concept can be widely accepted nowadays.

What I have just said implies that I identify the health of the humanities with their cognitive self-confidence. That is true, but it is only half the story. The health of a discipline as a discipline is entirely dependent upon the devoted allegiance of its members to the logic of inquiry. But the health of the humanities is also dependent upon their axiological self-confidence, their sense that they are pursuing *valuable* inquiry. It is just as important to distinguish these two kinds of health as it is to promote both. Indeed, I think we can have both only if we are capable of making this distinction. We humanists sometimes blur the distinction between value and knowledge just as we sometimes blur the one between rhetoric and knowledge. It is just as easy to know rigorously what is not worth knowing as it is to express with eloquent persuasiveness what is in fact nonsense. As I observed in chapter 6, some recent debates in literary theory have centered on whether the knowledge of a literary work can be separated from a judgment of its value, as though it were somehow impossible for two critics to understand meaning with equal accuracy and yet esteem it quite differently. But, of course, they can do this. The humanist's urge to conflate valuation and knowledge can be explained, but the explanation would be a digression from the issue at hand—which is the central importance of avoiding this confusion.

Why is it important? Without this confusion, we can redirect attention to the fact that a cognitive element inheres potentially in every field of the humanities, that the logic of this cognitive process is the same for all subject matters, and that this process of knowledge can be followed out on subjects of intense value or on subjects whose value will probably be very low, both now and in the future. The distinction between knowledge and value is important, therefore, to protect the integrity of inquiry in the humanities so that inquiry itself is not repudiated simply because some of its subject matters may have become trivial. The distinction is important, too, because it encourages a choice of those subject matters that are not trivial and whose potential or actual value is high.

This has come to be well understood in the natural sciences, where decisions about the probable value of inquiry involve immense allocations of money and human talent, both of which are limited. It is perfectly true that the future value of any inquiry is an unknown, and this is the most powerful argument for total freedom of inquiry. On the other hand, if we were not able to make shrewd predictions about the future value of an inquiry, we could not award the research grants available in the humanities. And, in a sense, each humanist awards himself his own research grant when he decides what professional projects he will pursue in the time available to him. The logical integrity of inquiry is a machine of fatalism, but the choice of inquiry is potentially free and need not be determined by a drift in the currents of intellectual fashion. This is why a demand that humanists make an accounting is a potential source of axiological health for the humanities.

Of course, the demand could be barbaric—especially when made by ideologues. Clearly, many aspects, valuable aspects, of humanistic knowledge do not bear even indirectly on racism or social justice. The demand for the immediate relevance of every aspect of humanistic inquiry is just as mindless and self-defeating as the demand for immediate applicability in the natural sciences. Yet surely the immediacy of problems (such as the decline of writing ability) does not *disqualify* them as subjects of inquiry, and the concept of "pure" research is overrated if no one can predict how such research could possibly be valuable. If the prediction cannot be made, then the likelihood that the inquiry will ever be valuable is clearly reduced, even though it may in fact turn out to be of great moment. No one will inhibit a humanist (since he does not need a big laboratory) from pursuing whatever happens to interest him. But if he cannot foresee potential value in his work, according to whatever value scheme he honors, then he should not be surprised if his work turns out to have small value.

The value of interpretation lies in its *application*—to recall from chapter 2 the old hermeneutic distinction between *interpretatio* and *applicatio*. The job of criticism is both to illuminate meaning (when necessary) and to indicate some valuable application of meaning, some special charm or use or wisdom for the present time. Ultimately, then, the aim of interpretation is to form a reliable basis for application. The value of knowledge is realized in its application, and there alone, even when the application resides in the spiritual exaltation of a pure contemplation of meaning. Exaltation is not a trivial value.

In chapter 8 I proposed that literary criticism since the nineteenth century has sometimes gone wrong by fusing and confusing literature-in-itself with literature as value-for-persons. A presiding tendency since Schiller and Coleridge, for instance, has been to insist that aesthetical terms like *form, richness, complex unity*, and *being interesting* are more adequate to criticism than the older, timeworn principle that literature should please or instruct, and, at its best, do both. Now, of the aesthetical terms mentioned above, the only one that directly connects literary value with value-for-persons is that of Henry James—*being interesting*. James's celebrated essay "The Art of Fiction" is significant in assuming from the start that fiction justifies itself not just by being well done and reflecting a fine sensibility, but also by being interesting and true. That is another way of saying that fiction should please and instruct. If a critic like Wayne Booth objects that the unreliable narrator in James's fiction makes its instruction ineffective, that objection, whether or not one judges it to be correct, is in perfect accord with the aims that James set

for fiction. Literature should please and instruct. That old for-
mula is more adequate to the character of literary value than
many another up-to-date critical formulation.

James's excellent essay reaffirms that the value of fiction largely
depends upon its truth—its human truth. Besides pleasing,
fiction and poetry ought to yield some kind of truth. Many
modern defenders of literature rightly claim for literature a kind
of truth not usually found in other modes of discourse—vivid
truths about human nature and emotion, about the forms of
human desire and the forms of resistance to human desire.
Literature instructs still by being true. Fiction has value beyond
the pleasure it gives, only because it presents something that is
not fiction. One of the chief values of fiction lies in the *knowledge* that it yields.

But fiction yields this knowledge only when it presents itself
under its true colors. The recent critical doctrine of criticism-as-
fiction or -poetry is a libel on good fiction or poetry. Fiction
which presents itself in the guise of scholarly textual commentary is a deception that yields no reliable knowledge. No English
or American adherent to this French theory has yet produced a
textual commentary under a fair-labeling statute, with a dis-
claimer stating: "This criticism is a work of fiction; any resemblance between its interpretations and the author's meanings are
purely coincidental." That would certainly reduce sales. And if
the name of the original text maker (Keats, Racine, etc.) were
omitted as a coauthor of the interpreted meanings, sales would
drop still lower. Nobody is instructed by fictions which are
merely fictions.

Like fiction and poetry, the humanities have greatest value
when they aim at knowledge. The knowledge they provide is
greatest when humanists accept both the cognitive and valuative
sides of humanistic study, without confusing them. Only when
humanists conceive one of their separate aims as *scientia*, a
communal and progressive cognitive enterprise, can the humanities have much value. Poets and fiction writers have generally admired literary scholars more than literary critics, on the

assumption that scholars give what all the best writers give—
permanently useful knowledge. On the other hand, evaluative
criticism can be of great importance at a particular time, more
valuable, in that historical context, than pure *scientia*. Yet,
without *scientia*, humanistic evaluation is empty and pointless.
That which humanists recover, understand, and preserve needs
to be preserved intact. To be useful, humanistic study, like any
other study, needs to be believed.

# Notes

## Chapter 1

1. "Objective Interpretation," *PMLA* 75 (September 1960): 463–79.
2. Reprinted in B. Lang and F. Williams, eds., *Marxism and Art*, trans. F. Williams (New York, 1972), pp. 249–50.
3. See chapter 2, pp. 30–31.
4. "For his part Heidegger made it clear that for him the stumbling blocks in Husserl's philosophy consisted in the transcendental reduction as 'bracketing of Being,' in the 'reduction' of man to pure consciousness, and finally, in the 'reduction' of Being into Being-object-for." J. J. Kockelmans, *Phenomenology* (New York, 1967), p. 274. See also Herbert Spiegelberg, *The Phenomenological Movement: A Historical Introduction*, 2 vols. (The Hague, 1960).
5. *Validity*, pp. 24–25.

## Chapter 2

1. Relativism in Heidegger and Gadamer is mainly historical relativism. A key phrase in Gadamer is "the historicity of understanding." See *Wahrheit und Methode* (Tübingen, 1960), a learned work that reinterprets the tradition of Schleiermacher in Heideggerian terms.
2. August Boeckh, *Encyclopädie und Methodologie der philologischen Wissenschaften* (Leipzig, 1877), pp. 11–12.
3. Ibid., p. 14.
4. Except for Humpty Dumpty in *Alice in Wonderland*, no semantic theorist I know of has been a pure intuitionist, nor do I know of any important theorist who has been a pure positivist. I describe the pure positions for the sake of clarity and also, more to the point, to show why a choice between them is logically required at some stage, even in an eclectic theory.
5. J. L. Austin, *How to Do Things with Words* (Oxford: Oxford University Press, 1962).
6. J. R. Searle, *Speech Acts* (Cambridge: Cambridge University Press, 1969).

7. H. P. Grice, "Meaning," *Philosophical Review*, July 1957, pp. 377–88, and later essays.

8. See chapter 3.

9. C. E. Bazell, "The Correspondence Fallacy in Structural Linguistics," in E. Hamp, ed., *Readings in Linguistics* (Chicago: University of Chicago Press, 1966).

10. Jean Piaget, *The Construction of Reality in the Child*, trans. M. Cook (New York, 1955), pp. 57–58.

11. D. L. Bolinger, "The Atomization of Meaning," *Language* 41 (1965): 555–73.

12. See, for instance, D. S. Boomer, "Hesitation and Grammatical Encoding," *Language and Speech* 8 (1965): 148–58.

## Chapter 3

1. Jean Piaget, *The Construction of Reality in the Child* (New York, 1971).

2. The inference that Kant's philosophy lay behind this conception is further supported by the suggestive fact that S. T. Coleridge, one of the first Englishmen to read Kant, was also the first author recorded in the *NED* to use the phrase "point of view" as a spiritual metaphor. On the other hand, David Hume showed himself to be a proto-Kantian in ways beyond those recognized by Kant, in the following use of the phrase, not recorded in the *NED*: "Every work of art in order to produce its due effect on the mind, must be surveyed in a certain point of view, and cannot be fully relished by persons whose situation, real or imaginary, is not conformable to that which is required by the performance" ("Of the Standard of Taste," 1757).

3. F. Meinecke, *Die Entstehung des Historismus* (Munich, 1947).

4. Bruno Snell, *The Discovery of the Mind*, trans. Rosenmeyer (Cambridge, Mass., 1953): "Homer's men had as yet no knowledge of the intellect or of the soul" (p. ix); "The Homeric man had a body exactly like the later Greeks, but he did not know it *qua* body, but merely as the sum total of his limbs. This is another way of saying that the Homeric Greeks did not yet have a body in the modern sense of the word" (p. 8).

5. H. G. Gadamer, *Wahrheit und Methode* (Tübingen, 1960), esp. pp. 290–324, and Roland Barthes, *Sur Racine* (Paris 1960).

6. Erich Auerbach, "Vico and Aesthetic Historicism," in *Scenes from the Drama of European Literature* (New York, 1959).

7. W. Dilthey, *Zergliedende und Beschreibende Psychologie*, vol. 5 in Gesammelete Schriften, 8 vols. (Berlin, 1921–31).

8. W. Dilthey, "The Dream," in W. Kluback, *Wilhelm Dilthey's Philosophy of History*, pp. 103-9.

9. Ch. Balley, *Linguistique générale et linguistique française* (Bern, 1944), p. 37. See also P. F. Strawson, "Intention and Convention in Speech Acts," *Philosophical Review* 73 (1964): 439–60.

## Chapter 4

1. The epistemological version is stated, for instance, in Ernst Cassirer's admirable work, *The Philosophy of Symbolic Forms*, vol. 1, *Language* (New Haven, 1953), especially pp. 249–95, and of course by disciples of Cassirer. I would like to believe that this chapter casts doubt on the necessarily constitutive character of particular symbolic forms.

2. See *Language, Thought and Reality* (Cambridge, Mass., 1956), especially pp. 134–59. Whorf implied that perfect synonomy and inter-translatability is possible within the European group of languages which he called "SAE" for "Standard Average European." But this concession presents a logical difficulty for arguing the impossibility of synonymy or inter-translatability between languages of different types. For, if synonymity can occur within a language group, despite differences of form, the diverse formal features of disparate languages would not in themselves prevent synonymy. Cultural rather than linguistic differences might indeed temporarily do so, but that is another matter. It is notable that psycholinguistic researches do not support Whorf's assumption of an isomorphism of form and content. See, for instance, H. Hörman, *Psycholinguistics*, trans. H. Stern (New York, 1971). Hörman finds that preverbal thought does not necessarily "contain a temporal organization." Its schemata often lack "temporal valence" (p. 249). This point, of course, touches on the form of language, but does not dispute the constitutive character of certain linguistic categories.

3. This should not be taken as an argument for the indeterminacy of linguistic meaning itself. Quite the contrary; it is because meaning can be stable and determinate despite variations in mental acts and linguistic forms that the relation between form and meaning must be indeterminate on the basis merely of rules and conventions.

4. *Through the Looking Glass*, ch. 6.

5. Peter Heath, ed., *The Philosopher's Alice* (New York, 1974), p. 193.

6. J. L. Austin, *How to Do Things with Words* (Oxford, 1962).

7. For bibliographical references to these discussions, the reader is referred to the excellent article by Leonard Linsky, "Synonymity," in *Encyclopedia of Philosophy*, 8 vols. (New York, 1967), vol. 8.

8. I recognize that 2 is not necessarily always synonymous with 1 + 1. My claim is that the two expressions can be synonymous in an actual use.

9. F. H. Bradley, *The Principles of Logic* (Oxford, 1928), pp. 141–42. Reprinted in I. M. Copi and J. A. Gould, eds., *Readings on Logic* (New York, 1964).

10. Though some theorists, notably Chomsky, have questioned the standard classifications of linguistic levels, that debate over description does not affect my argument stressing the functional variability of linguistic elements, however they be described.

11. The variable functionality of stylistic traits is the implicit caveat

behind intelligent stylistic analysis, as Leo Spitzer (and Spitzer alone, I believe, among theorists of style) was willing to concede: "A metaphor, an anaphora, a staccato rhythm may be found anywhere in literature; they may or may not be significant. What tells us they are is only the feeling, which we must already have acquired, for the whole of the particular work of art." *Linguistics and Literary History* (Princeton, 1948), p. 29.

12. Roger Brown, *Words and Things* (New York, 1958), pp. 229–63.

13. See, for instance, James Deese, *The Structure of Association in Language and Thought* (Baltimore, 1965); Roger Brown, and Donald Hildman, "Expectancy and the Perception of Syllables," *Language* vol. 32 (1956); P. N. Johnson-Laird, "The Perception and Memory of Sentences," and D. B. Fry, "Speech Reception and Perception," both in J. Lyons, ed., *New Horizons in Linguistics* (Baltimore, 1970).

14. C. E. Bazell, *Linguistic Form* (Istanbul, 1953).

15. "The Sememe," reprinted in Hamp, Householder, and Austerlitz, *Readings in Linguistics II* (Chicago, 1966), pp. 334, 336.

16. "The Sememe," p. 339.

17. See Wayne Booth, *The Rhetoric of Irony* (Chicago, 1974), p. 51: "Irony thus often produces a much higher degree of confidence than literal statement."

18. See P. Ziff, "The Nonsynonymy of Active and Passive Sentences," *Philosophical Review* 75 (1966): 226–32, and J. J. Katz and E. Martin, "The Synonymy of Actives and Passives," *Philosophical Review* 76 (1967): 476–91.

19. Roy Harris, *Synonymy and Linguistic Analysis* (Oxford, 1973).

20. See G. J. Warnock, "John Langshaw Austin: A Biographical Sketch," in K. T. Fann, ed., *Symposium on J. L. Austin* (London, 1969).

21. *Philosophical Investigations* (New York, 1953), p. 11E. In this passage I have altered Ms. Anscombe's translation of *Zeichen* from "symbols" to "signs."

22. See H. P. Grice, "Utterer's Meaning, Sentence-Meaning, and Word-Meaning," in *Foundations of Language* 4 (1968): 225–42. P. F. Strawson, "Intention and Convention in Speech-Acts," *Philosophical Review* 73 (1964): 439–60. J. R. Searle, *Speech Acts* (Cambridge, 1969). Max Black, "Meaning and Intention: An Examination of Grice's Views," *New Literary History* 4 (1973): 257–79.

23. Black, "Meaning and Intention," p. 257.

24. P. F. Strawson, *Meaning and Truth* (Oxford, 1970), pp. 7–9.

25. Leonard Linsky, *Referring* (London, 1967), esp. pp. 116–31.

26. Alonzo Church, "Propositions," *Encyclopedia Britannica* (1971), 18:640.

27. Paul Marhenke, "The Criterion of Significance," in L. Linsky, ed., *Semantics and the Philosophy of Language* (Urbana, 1952), p. 146.

## Chapter 5

1. F. D. E. Schleiermacher, *Hermeneutik*, ed. Heinz Kimmerle (Heidelberg, 1959), p. 90. The original reads: "Alles was noch einer näheren Bestimmung bedarf in einer gegebene Rede, darf nur aus dem dem Verfasser und seinem ursprünglichen Publikum gemeinsamen Sprachgebiet bestimmt werden."

2. The structure of this distinction I owe to the writings of Husserl whose influence I acknowledge in the earlier piece alluded to, "Objective Interpretation," *PMLA* 75 (September 1960).

3. This is a shorthand, not a pejorative term which comprises all non-authorial meaning, whether or not such meaning was possible within "the linguistic domain common to the author and his original public." I use the term in preference to "non-authorial meaning" because the chief disputes have centered, as Schleiermacher's canon suggests, on the question of historicity. Either term would serve.

4. Augustus De Morgan, "On the Structure of the Syllogism and on the Application of the Theory of Probabilities to Questions of Argument and Authority," *Cambridge Philosophical Transactions* (November 9, 1846).

## Chapter 6

1. See Murray Krieger, "Literary Analysis and Evaluation and the Ambidextrous Critic," and Northrop Frye, "On Value Judgments"; both in L. S. Dembo, ed., *Criticism: Speculative and Analytical Essays* (Madison, Wis., 1968).

2. *Anatomy of Criticism* (Princeton, 1957), pp. 7–8.

3. René Wellek and Austin Warren, *Theory of Literature*, 3d ed. (New York, 1956), p. 156.

4. See especially his essay "Beauty and Aesthetic Value," *Journal of Philosophy* 59 (1962): 617–28.

5. *Concepts of Criticism*, ed. Stephen G. Nichols, Jr. (New Haven, 1963), p. 52.

6. *Critique of Judgment*, sec. 7. Quotations from this work, cited by section, are based on (but do not in every case precisely follow) the excellent new translation by Walter Cerf, ed., *Analytic of the Beautiful*, The Library of Liberal Arts (Indianapolis, 1963).

7. Sec. 20. Thus Kant: "Nur unter Voraussetzung, sage ich, eines solchen Gemeinsinns kann das Geschmacksurteil gefällt werden." *Kritik der Urteilskraft*, ed. K. Vorländer (Leipzig, 1924).

8. For a recent discussion and account of previous work on "affective meaning" see John Parry, *The Psychology of Human Communication* (London, 1967), pp. 65–69, 212–17.

## Chapter 7

1. J. W. Lenz, ed., *On the Standard of Taste and Other Essays* (Indianapolis, 1965), p. 7.

2. Ibid.

3. See his essay "The Literary Influence of Academies."

4. J. Shawcross, ed., *Biographia Literaria*, 2 vols. (1907), 1:44.

5. E. L. Griggs, ed., *Collected Letters of Samuel Taylor Coleridge: Volume II, 1801–1806* (Oxford, 1956), p. 864. (To W. Sotheby, Sept. 10, 1802: "Nature has her proper interest; & he will know what it is, who believes and feels, that every Thing has a Life of its own, & that we are all *one Life.*")

6. The exhaustiveness of the scheme is deduced as follows: Works are valued on criteria that are either (1) intrinsic, or (2) extrinsic. Extrinsic value criteria are defined as being disparate from the aims of the author or of the work. Intrinsic criteria are defined as constituting the implicit aims of the author or the work. The three types of "intrinsic" criteria that have been advanced are (1) *sui generis* criteria, restricted to the individual work; (2) specific criteria, limited to the species or sub-genre to which the work belongs; (3) broadly generic criteria, restricted to a large genus that includes many different species of works, but excludes some species. To go beyond (3), admitting without restriction any type of criteria, would be to collapse into the extrinsic. This analytical scheme, though exhaustive, is of course itself unprivileged. It is designed for the purpose of discussing the claim of intrinsicality in evaluation. Different classificatory schemes of value-criteria might be more useful for other purposes. See, for instance, the four-fold scheme of Wayne Booth in *A Rhetoric of Irony* (Chicago, 1974), pp. 196–221.

7. *Principles of Literary Criticism* (New York, 1925), p. 71.

8. "The Critical Monism of Cleanth Brooks," in *Critics and Criticism Ancient and Modern*, ed. R. S. Crane (Chicago, 1952), pp. 83–107.

9. B. Croce, *Aesthetic as Science of Expression and General Linguistic*, trans. D. Ainslie, rev. ed. (New York, 1922), pp. 90, 92.

10. Ibid., p. 90.

11. See, more particularly, the application to criticism of Wittgenstein's observations in M. Weitz, *"Hamlet" and the Philosophy of Literary Criticism* (Chicago, 1964).

12. For documentation of this point, see R. Langbaum, "The Function of Criticsm Once More," in *Yale Review* 54 (1965): 205–18.

13. See Wayne Shumaker, *Elements of Critical Theory* (Berkeley, 1952). On this point I agree entirely with Professor Shumaker, who closes his book as follows: "Judgments rendered against any evaluative reference frame, no matter how trivial, will have something of the character of proved fact if only the reference frame is adequately acknowledged. Judgments rendered

against concealed standards, however, will always appear arbitrary and, to those unconvinced by rhetoric or authority, meaningless."

## Chapter 8

1. I. A. Richards, *Principles of Literary Criticism*, 2d ed. (1926), pp. 201–2, 204: "This reconciliation, this appeasement, is common to much good and to much bad poetry alike. But the value of it depends upon the level of organization at which it takes place, upon whether the reconciled impulses are adequate or inadequate." "We have to ask in applying the test what the responses in question are, and in the case of poetry they are so varied, so representative of all the activities of life, that actual universal preference on the part of those who have tried both kinds fairly is the same (on our view) as superiority of the one over the other. Keats, by universal qualified opinion, is a more efficient poet than Wilcox, and that is the same thing as saying that his works are more valuable."

2. The following three passages by Winters are from *Primitivism and Decadence* (1937), as reprinted in *In Defense of Reason* (New York, 1947) on pp. 22, 24, and 28 respectively: "The rather limp versification of Mr. Eliot and of Mr. MacLeish is inseparable from the spiritual limpness that one feels behind the poems." "Literary history is packed with sickening biographies. But it is worth noting that the poetry of such a man, say, as Rochester (who in this is typical of his age) displays a mastery of an extremely narrow range of experience." "It should be observed again how the moral discipline is involved in the literary discipline, how it becomes, at times, almost a matter of living philology."

These two passages from Leavis are in the Penguin edition of *The Great Tradition* (London, 1962), pp. 12 and 17 respectively: "There can't be subtlety of organization without richer matter to organize, and subtler interests than Fielding has to offer. He is credited with range and variety . . . . But we haven't to read a very large proportion of *Tom Jones* in order to discover the limits of the essential interests it has to offer us. Fielding's attitudes and his concern with human nature are simple." "When we examine the formal perfection of *Emma*, we find that it can be appreciated only in terms of the moral preoccupations that characterize the novelist's peculiar interest in life. Those who suppose it to be an 'aesthetic matter,' a beauty of 'composition' that is combined miraculously with 'truth to life,' can give no adequate reason for the view that *Emma* is a great novel, and no intelligent account of its perfection of form."

3. See *The Verbal Icon: Studies in the Meaning of Poetry* (Lexington, Ky., 1954). "The moral value in any given situation, what is right, is abstract; it is known by rule and conscience. By necessity it excludes. Neither a right nor a wrong choice, however, excludes the awareness of

many values, some interrelated and supporting, some rival, some sacrificed by a choice, some in some situations held in ironic balance or entering into unresolved tensions" (p. 98). "A poem, even a great poem, may fall short of being moral.... It is yet true that poems as empirically discovered and tested do tend within their limits and given the peculiar *données* or presuppositions of each, to point toward the higher integration of dogma" (p. 100). Wimsatt adheres to a system of values in which "poetic is distinguished from moral and both are understood in relation to the master ideas of evil as negation or not-being, a gap in order, and of good as positive, or being—in the natural order the *designed complexity* of what is most truly one or most has being" (p. 100; my italics).

4. Booth calls a big essay by McKeon "the fullest statement of the critical pluralism on which this book is based." *The Rhetoric of Fiction* (Chicago, 1961), p. 403.

5. *The Rhetoric of Fiction*, p. 138: "We may exhort ourselves to read tolerantly, we may quote Coleridge on the willing suspension of disbelief until we think ourselves totally suspended in a relativistic universe, and still we will find many books which postulate readers we refuse to become, books that depend on 'beliefs' or 'attitudes' ... which we cannot adopt even hypothetically as our own." And on p. 378: "Impersonal narration has raised moral difficulties too often for us to dismiss moral questions as irrelevant to technique."

6. "Though first-rate critics like Wilson, Empson, Trilling, and Burke have not hesitated to make 'extraliterary' sense of literature, the idea that we positively ought to do so is conceived as a threat to scholarly balance. The critic already knows what he is doing and will be all right if he can just keep himself from being overly drawn toward either what Frye has called 'the myth of concern' or the 'myth of detachment' " (in "Anaesthetic Criticism: I," *The New York Review of Books* 26 [February 1970]: p. 33). It has been said that Frye is more concerned with criticism as criticism than literature as literature. But criticism is an autonomous enterprise only under an intrinsic conception of literature that limits itself to certain kinds of writings or to certain special traits in writing. Otherwise Frye's theory of criticism would belong simply to psychology and anthropology, which it indeed does, willy-nilly, when it claims to make true, large-scale statements about the human mind.

7. "And as some of those who write about me are still asserting that I ignore the social reference of literary criticism, the sub-title calls the attention of those who read me to the fact that I have written about practically nothing else." *The Stubborn Structure; Essays on Criticism and Society* (London, 1970), p. x.

8. The following passages are from *Anatomy of Criticism* (Princeton, 1957), pp. 115, 119, and 122 respectively: "The archetypal view of literature shows us literature as a total form and literary experience as a part of the

continuum of life, in which one of the poet's functions is to visualize the goals of human work. As soon as we add this approach to the other three, literature becomes an ethical instrument, and we pass beyond Kierkegaard's 'Either / Or' dilemma between aesthetic idolatry and ethical freedom, without any temptation to dispose of the arts in the process. Hence the importance, after accepting the validity of this view of literature, of rejecting the external goals of morality, beauty, and truth. The fact that they are external makes them ultimately idolatrous, and so demonic." "When we pass into anagogy, nature becomes, not the container, but the thing contained, and the archetypal universal symbols, the city, the garden, the quest, the marriage, are no longer desirable forms that man constructs inside nature, but are themselves the forms of nature. Nature is now inside the mind of an infinite man who builds his cities out of the Milky Way." "The anagogic view of criticism thus leads to the conception of literature as existing in its own universe, no longer a commentary on life or reality, but containing life and reality in a system of verbal relationships."

9. *Anatomy*, p. 7: "If criticism exists, it must be an examination of literature in terms of a conceptual framework derivable from an inductive survey of the literary field."

10. See, for instance, Walter Sutton, *Modern American Criticism* (Englewood Cliffs, N.J., 1963), p. 289: "The most obvious need of critical theory today is the integration of aesthetic or formalist and social or historical considerations. Literature and criticism are social functions.... The critic and scholar will increasingly realize that he is socially engaged in all his activities. It is his obligation to keep criticism open to new ideas and values so that it may continue to provide fresh knowledge of an ever-expanding world of interrelated literary and social experience." The most trenchant statement I know of is in Robert Weimann, *"New Criticism" und die Entwicklung Bürgerlicher Literaturwissenschaft* (Halle, 1962), p. 131: "Die neukritische Grundanschauung vom Kunstwerk als einem in sich ruhenden Phänomen leugnet ja jede Beziehung zwischen Werk und Realität. Sie verwirft dreierlei: die historische Wirklichkeit, damit aber zugleich das Publikum und schliesslich auch den Künstler als Bezugspunkte der Dichtung. Dementsprechend ist auch ihre Frontstellung eine dreifache: sie wendet sich gegen das Aristotelische Prinzip der *mimesis* oder Nachahmung, gegen das Horazsche Prinzip *aut prodesse aut delectare* und schliesslich gegen die letzte von der Romantik geduldete und geförderte ausserästhetische Bestimmung—die biographische Beziehung zum Schöpfer des Werkes. Sie negiert also die abbildende-verallgemeinernde, die didaktischeunterhaltende, und die Ausdrucksfunktion der Kunst. Sie verwirft damit die Kunstanfassung der grössten Dichter der Vergangenheit."

11. Out of countless examples, take Leavis: "Literature will yield to the sociologist, or anyone else, what it has to give only if it is approached as literature." *The Common Pursuit* (London, 1952), p. 193.

12. See especially chaps. 3 and 4 of *What is Art?*

13. The principles of R. S. Crane, based on the formal requirements of *any* genre, can be so extended. Yet this would still remain a formal, technical approach, and thus "aesthetic" in the broad sense of the term. Moreover one can apply stylistic and other categories used in other forms of intrinsic criticism to any utterance, literary or nonliterary, with useful and appropriate results.

14. The first definition in the *OED* runs as follows: "Acquaintance with 'letters' or books; polite or humane learning; literary culture. Now *rare* and *obsolescent*. (The only sense in Johnson and Todd 1818.)"

15. See *The Collected Writings of Thomas de Quincey,* ed. David Masson, 14 vols. (Edinburgh, 1890), 10:46: "The word *literature* is a perpetual source of confusion, because it is used in two senses, and those senses liable to be confused with each other. In a philosophical use of the word, Literature is the direct and adequate antithesis of Books of Knowledge. But in popular use it is a mere term of convenience for expressing inclusively the total books of a language" (from "Letters to a Young Man etc.," 1823). He took up the attempt again in 1847 (11:53): "What is it that we mean by *literature?* Popularly, and amongst the thoughtless, it is held to include everything that is printed in a book.... Not only is much that takes a station in books not literature; but inversely much that really *is* literature never reaches a station in books. The weekly sermons of Christendom, that vast pulpit literature which acts so extensively upon the popular mind—to warn, to uphold, to renew, to comfort, to alarm—does not attain the sanctuary of libraries in the ten-thousandth part of its extent." (To this de Quincey appends a note excluding the "Blue Books" of Parliamentary statistics from the honorary classification.)

16. *Biographia Literaria,* ed. Shawcross, 2 vols. (Oxford, 1907), 1:26: "Now it is no less remarkable than true with how little examination works of polite literature are commonly pursued." And on p. 159: "But woefully will that man find himself mistaken who imagines that the profession of literature or (to speak more plainly) the *trade* of authorship, besets its members with fewer or with less insidious temptations than the church, the law, or the different branches of commerce."

17. See *The Complete Works of William Hazlitt in Twenty-One Volumes, Vol. 16: Contributions to the Edinburgh Review,* ed. P. P. Howe (London, 1933), pp. 318–37. The title is "American Literature—Dr. Channing." It is a review of *Sermons and Tracts* (1829) and ranks Channing with Irving, Cooper, and Brown.

18. Voltaire's view is similar to de Quincey's of 1847: "Le mot ouvrage de la littérature ne convient point à un livre qui enseigne l'architecture ou la musique, les fortifications, la castramétation, etc.; c'est un ouvrage technique." Quoted by Paul Robert under "littérature" in *Dictionnaire alphabétique et analogique de la langue française: les mots et les associations d'idées,* 6 vols. (Paris, 1966), 4:124–25.

19. "Terme général, qui désigne l'érudition, la connaissance des Belles Lettres, & des matières qui y ont rapport. Voyez le mot LETTRES, où en faisant leur éloge on a démontré leur intime union avec les Sciences proprement dites." Vol. 9 of *Encyclopédie ou dictionnaire raisonné des sciences des arts et des metiers* (Neuchâtel, 1765).

20. Roger Brown, *Words and Things* (Glencoe, Ill., 1958), pp. 229–53.

21. René Wellek, *Concepts of Criticism*, ed. S. G. Nichols (New Haven, 1963), p. 31: "While in France Sainte-Beuve re-established the supremacy of the critic as a public figure and in England Matthew Arnold made criticism the key to modern culture and the salvation of England, in Germany criticism lost status drastically."

22. Richard Green Moulton, *The Bible as Literature* (London, 1899). This began as a university syllabus, published in 1891, under the title *Syllabus: The Literary Study of the Bible.*

23. See chapter 7, "Privileged Criteria in Evaluation."

24. This is a recurring topos or archetype of intrinsic criticism. As late as 1957 Frye was stating: "It is clear that the absence of systematic criticism has created a power vacuum, and all the neighboring disciplines have moved in" (*Anatomy*, p. 12).

25. These pronouncements, which follow Plato's views in the *Laws*, are subjects for further study rather than self-evident truths. The subjects have not been carefully studied. Even after you have won provisional agreement about the nature of a good or bad effect, you will still need to find out empirically, in a given cultural situaiton, what the *predominant* effect of a work (or a fashion) actually is. Students of literature need not leave this empirical work to others; it falls under the "literary study of literature" just as much as aesthetic inquiries do. "Minor" works of art like Mrs. Sherwood's *The Fairchild Family* are said to have twisted influential minds of a whole age, not because the books were technically bad, but precisely because they were technically (artistically) effective and thereby all the more pernicious. In the absence of careful empirical studies of effects, we are well advised to follow Plato and not prejudge the issue with a middle category "art" that magically fuses the technically effective and the morally good.

26. Johan Huizinga, *Men and Ideas* (New York, 1959), p. 245.

## Chapter 9

1. Here, for example, is a succinct statement by Goethe on the subject of historical knowledge:

> Die Zeiten der Vergangenheit
> Sind uns ein Buch mit sieben Siegeln.
> Was ihr den Geist der Zeiten heisst,

Das ist im Grund der Herren eigner Geist,
In dem die Zeiten sich bespiegeln.
                              *Faust*, I, ll. 575–79.

2. T. S. Kuhn, *The Structure of Scientific Revolutions*, 2d ed. (Chicago: University of Chicago Press, 1970), p. 209.

3. Karl Popper, "Normal Science and its Dangers," in *Criticism and the Growth of Knowledge*, ed. I. Lakatos and A. Musgrave (Cambridge: Cambridge University Press, 1970), pp. 56–57. My italics.

# Index

Addison, Joseph, 110
Aesthetic criteria, 121, 134, 135
Aesthetic values, overemphasis on, 12
Aestheticism, 138, 140
Aesthetics, 98–109, 116, 131
Affect, 108
"Affective Meaning," 103
Ainslie, Douglas, 164
Alice (Lewis Carroll), as linguistic theorist, 51, 52, 71; contrasted with Humpty Dumpty, 68
Allegory, 23, 77, 85
Amyot, Jacques, 141, 142
Anachronism, 77, 82, 83, 85, 88, 89
Analyticity, 53–58
Anti-rationalism, 13
Anti-separatism (value and description), 98
*Applicatio* contrasted with *interpretatio,* 19, 87
Approach, concept of, 42–44, 74, 148
Archimedes, 42
Aristotle, 43, 67, 111, 113–16, 118–21, 130, 138, 142
Arnold, Matthew, 43, 111, 115, 121, 133, 139, 142, 169
*Ars explicandi,* 19
*Ars intelligendi,* 19
Art, 116
Auerbach, Erich, 41, 160, 162
Austin, J. L., 25, 26, 52, 53, 67, 68, 159, 161

Authenticity, 45
Author's intention, 11, 79. *See also* Intention; Original meaning
Authority (interpretive norm), 111
Autonomy (as goal of a discipline), 137

Bacon, Francis, 18
Balance as classical and Arnoldian ideal, 139
Balley, Charles, 160
Barth, Karl, 45
Barthes, Roland, 39, 41, 88, 89, 91
Bazell, C. E., 29, 65, 66, 67, 160 162
Beardsley, Monroe, 98
Beauty: concept of, 98, 101, 105, 117, 131; theory of, 98–109, 116, 131
Bentley, Richard, 89
Berkeley, George, 142
Bible, 20
Black, Max, 68, 69, 71, 162
Blake, William, 23
Boeckh, August, 17, 18, 159
Bolinger, D. L., 33, 160
*Bonnes lettres,* 141, 144
Boomer, D. S., 160
Booth, Wayne, 122, 125, 126, 156, 162, 164, 166
Bracketing in phenomenology, 3–6
Bradley, F. H., 55, 161
Bradley, Henry, 60
Brentano, Franz, 48

Broad-genre criteria (in evaluation),
   116–18
Brooks, Cleanth, 117, 164
Brown, Charles Brockden, 168
Brown, Roger, 62, 162, 169
Bultmann, Rudolf, 45
Bunyan, John, 110
Burke, Kenneth, 166
Butler, Joseph, 142

Canons of interpretation, 20
Carlyle, Thomas, 42
Carnap, Rudolf, 54
Carroll, Lewis, 52
Cassirer, Ernst, 161
Categories: Kantian, 48, 49; in
   literary criticism, 134
Catholicism, 21
Cerf, Walter, 163
Channing, William Ellery, 132, 168
Chaucer, 40
Chomsky, Noam, 161
Chuang Tzu, 69
Church, Alonzo, 73, 162
Clauses, verbal, 56
Cleaver, Eldridge, 140
Cognition, 100, 103, 106; in the
   humanities, 154
Cognitive atheism, 4, 36, 49
Coleridge, S. T., 43, 75, 90, 111–
   14, 116, 119, 120, 132, 138, 156,
   160, 164, 166
Collins, Churton, 141, 142
Collins, William, 142
Common sense (term in Kant's
   philosophy), 99
Community of inquiry, 152, 153
Complexity as literary criterion,
   117, 121, 125
Compression as literary criterion,
   121
Composition, teaching of, 144
Consciousness, 76
Constitution, the, 20
Context, linguistic, 3, 58

Conventions, linguistic, 10, 26, 34,
   50, 68, 69, 70, 71, 85
Cooper, J. F., 168
Copi, I. M., 161
Corrigible schemata, 33, 34
Crane, R. S., 117, 129, 168
Crews, F., 91, 126
Criticism: as fiction, 147, 157; as
   poetry, 157
Croce, Benedetto, 67, 116–21, 164
Cultural categories (Kantian), 46,
   47, 48, 101
Cultural objects, 102, 109

Darwin, Charles, 60, 142
Decadence of literary study, 13
Decontextualization in writing, 60
Deese, James, 62, 162
Definition, aristotelian, 121
Defoe, Daniel, 24, 25
De Gourmont, Rémy, 138
Dembo, L. S., 163
De Morgan, Augustus, 84, 163
De Quincey, Thomas, 132, 168
Derrida, Jacques, 13, 147
Descartes, René, 142
Determinacy of meaning, 1, 3
Dialects, 28, 64
Dickens, Charles, 134
Diderot, Denis, 132
*Différence*, 147
Dilthey, Wilhelm, 5, 17, 35, 41–44,
   46, 150, 151, 160
Disciplines, humanistic, 152. *See
   also* Humanities
Dogmatic relativism, 9. *See also*
   Relativism
Double perspective, 49
Dowden, Edward, 141, 142
Dürer, Albrecht, 37

Eliot, T. S., 87, 134, 165
Emotion, in meaning, 103, 108
Empson, William, 166

*Episteme*, 147, 148
Erasmus, 141, 142
*Erklären* contrasted with *Verstehen*, 150
Essex, Second Earl of, 88
Ethical principles of interpretation, 7, 8, 85, 89, 90, 92, 135, 139
Etymology, 56
Euripides, 118
Evaluation, 95–109, 110–23; contrasted with interpretation, 11
Evidence, 151, 152, 153, 154
Extrinsic criteria in criticism, 113, 114, 115, 122

Fallacy of the homogeneous past, 40
Fallacy of the homogeneous present, 41
Fallacy of the inscrutable past, 39
Fann, K. T., 162
Fielding, Henry, 165
Form as opposed to content in speech, 10, 50, 57, 71, 156
Formalism, 124
Foucault, Michel, 148
Framework, myth of, 147
Freedom of inquiry, 155
Freud, Sigmund, 43, 81
Fry, D. B., 162
Frye, Northrop, 11, 95, 96, 126, 129, 163, 166

Gadamer, H. G., 17, 39, 40, 49, 159, 160
Genres, 33, 35, 67, 119, 120, 133
Generic criteria, 115, 118, 120
Glossematics, 66
Gödel, Kurt, 50, 66
Goethe, J. W. von, 169
Goldmann, Lucien, 2
Gombrich, E. H., 32
Goodman, Nelson, 54
Gould, J. A., 161
Gray, Thomas, 142

Grice, H. P., 26, 54, 68, 69, 71, 160, 162
Griggs, E. L., 164
Guizot, François, 42

Hamp, Eric, 162
Harris, Roy, 67, 162
Hazlitt, William, 132, 168
Heath, Peter, 52, 161
Heidegger, Martin, 4–6, 13, 17, 19, 31, 32, 35, 81–85, 159
Heraclitus, 42
Herder, J. G. von, 38, 41, 78
Hermeneutic circle, 6, 9, 10, 81, 82, 83
Hermeneutics, 74, 79, 81, 84; analytical dimension, 89; biblical, 9, 18, 20; canons in, 22; descriptive and normative dimensions, 75, 95; ethical choice in, 78; etymology of, 18; general, 9, 17, 18; hypotheses in, 33, 34; legal, 20, 22; legitimacy in, 76, 77; local, 18; normative dimension, 78; positivism in, 22, 23, 25; skepticism in, 10, 27, 36
Hermes, 18
Hesitation phenomena in speech, 33
Hildman, Donald, 162
Historical reconstruction, 83
Historical relativism, 36
Historicism, 27, 38–42, 77, 78, 99
Historicity, 83; of understanding, 81, 159
Homer, 76, 77, 108, 134
Horizon in phenomenology, 2
*Horizontverschmelzung*, 49
Hörman, H., 161
Householder, Fred, 162
Howe, P. P., 168
Humanities, 12, 72, 109, 137, 147, 149, 151, 153, 154
Hume, David, 110–12, 142, 160
Humpty Dumpty as linguistic theorist, 51, 56, 71, 159

Huizinga, Johan, 140, 169
Husserl, Edmund, 2, 4, 5, 29, 35, 48, 159, 163
Hypotheses, 35, 151–54

Ideology, 147, 148, 149
*Iliad*, 39, 108
Illocutionary force, 26, 52, 53, 67
Implied author, 6
Implied speaker, 6
Indeterminacy in speech, 64, 71, 161
Ingarden, Roman, 129
Instrumental effects of literature, 126
Intention, 8, 33, 69, 70, 71, 87, 90, 119; allied with convention in speech, 68
Intentional acts and objects, 8
Intentionality of Consciousness, 4, 48
Intentional fallacy, 118
*Interpretatio* contrasted with *applicatio*, 19, 156
Interpretation, 20, 74, 75, 76, 79. *See also* Hermeneutics
Intrinsic criticism, 115, 117, 118, 124, 126, 127, 129, 144. *See also* New Criticism
Intrinsic valuation, 113
Intuitionism, 21, 23, 26, 33, 34
Irony, 23, 107
Irving, Washington, 168

James, Henry, 156
Jansenism, 2
Jespersen, Otto, 60
Johnson, Samuel, 43, 107, 115, 121, 131, 168
Johnson-Laird, P. N., 162
Jung, C. G., 43

Kant, Immanuel, 4, 9, 11, 37, 38, 42, 45, 46, 48, 90, 95, 160, 163;

*Critique of Judgment*, 98–109; *Critique of Pure Reason*, 101
Katz, J. J., 162
Kayser, Wolfgang, 129
Keats, John, 104, 105, 157, 165
Kierkegaard, Sören, 140, 167
Kimmerle, Heinz, 163
Kluback, W., 160
Knowledge in interpretation and humanistic study, 1, 72, 73, 96, 108, 123, 146, 149, 152, 153, 157, 158
Kockelmans, J. J., 159
Kott, Jan, 41
Krieger, Murray, 95, 163
Kuhn, Thomas, 148, 152, 170

Lakatos, I., 170
Lang, B., 159
Langbaum, Robert, 164
Language, 148
Leavis, F. R., 43, 125, 126, 165, 167
*Lebenswelt*, 101
Legal codes, 131
Legitimacy of extrinsic criteria, 117
Lenz, 164
Lexicography, 60
Linguistic asymmetry, principle of, 29, 57
Linguistic determinism, doctrine of, 51, 53
Linguistic rules, 26, 34, 50, 69
Linguistics, 65, 103
Linsky, Leonard, 54, 161, 162
Literature, 75, 116, 124; as art, 12, 109, 130; canon of, 140; as discourse, 91, 142; heterogeneity of, 136; historical definitions of, 131–35; as literature, 113, 114, 123, 125, 129, 130; ontic status of, 137; undefinability of, 135
Literary criteria, broad genre, 116, 117, 118

Literary study, 128, 136, 137, 144, 149
Literary theory, 59, 75, 87, 90, 96, 103
Logic of inquiry, 151, 152, 154
Luther, Martin, 111
Lyons, John, 162

MacLeish, Archibald, 165
Making-matching process in interpretation, 32, 33
Mannheim, Karl, 147
Marhenke, Paul, 162
Martin, E., 162
Marx, Karl, 43
Marxism, 44, 147
Masson, David, 168
Mates, Benson, 54
Maturity, literary criterion of, 117, 121, 123
McKeon, Richard, 166
Meaning, 69, 72, 76, 87; correlation with value, 8, 104; determinacy of, 1, 3, 6; opposed to significance, 1–13, 79–81, 85, 86, 146; stability of, 3, 4, 6, 146; as use, 25, 62
Meaning expectations, 32, 35, 63
Meinecke, Friederich, 38, 160
Meinong, Alexius von, 48
Memory, 48
Mental set, 101–8. *See also* Subjective stance
Metaphysics in hermeneutics, 81, 83, 84
Methodological perspectivism, 42–44
Methodology in interpretation, 17, 50, 71, 72, 96
Middle axioms, 18
Mill, J. S., 142, 150
Milton, John, 76
Mixed criteria in criticism, 11, 12, 124–45

Model, 35
Montaigne, Michel de, 141
Moral criticism of literature, 121, 125
Morphemes, 57, 64
Moulton, R. G., 133, 169
Musgrave, A., 170

Natural science, 96, 149, 151
Neo-Kantianism, 150
New Criticism, 87, 121, 124, 126, 127, 128, 129, 130
Nichols, S. G., Jr., 163, 169
Nominalism, 121

Objectivism, 17
*Odyssey*, 39
Oldmixion, John, 24
Organic unity, 111
Original meaning, 79, 88, 89, 92

Pap, Arthur, 54
Paradigm, 147–49
Paradox as literary criterion, 117
Parry, John, 163
Pascal, Blaise, 2
Pater, Walter, 142
Perspectivism, 9, 10, 27, 28, 30, 31, 36–49, 148
Phenomenological brackets, 3–6
Phenomenology, 101
Philology, 60, 128
Phoneme, 28, 29, 32, 57, 65, 79
Phonetics, 28
Piaget, Jean, 3, 30, 31, 32, 35, 37, 160
Picard, Raymond, 88, 89, 91
Plato, 42, 43, 51, 108, 114, 115, 116, 122, 137, 138, 140, 169
Poetry as poetry, 59, 113, 116, 129, 130
Polite letters, 133
Popper, Karl, 170
Positivism, 26, 33

Pre-accommodation, 82
Priority of cognition, 100–101
Probability, 2, 151–53
Proposition, 72, 73, 154
Prose, 142–43
Protestantism, 21
Psycholinguistics, 61–62
Psychologism, 4, 27, 28, 31

Quine, W. O. van, 54

Rabelais, François, 141
Racine, Jean, 2, 41, 45, 46, 88, 89, 157
Ranke, Leopold von, 78
Raphael, 42–43
Reader as Author, 49
Re-cognition, 3, 106
Relational theory of value, 97–98
Relativism, 3, 4, 5, 9, 12, 13, 17, 37, 49, 147, 148
Relevance as literary criterion, 155
Rhetoric in the humanities, 153–54
Richards, I. A., 115, 125, 126, 129, 165
Richness as literary criterion, 121
Rickert, Heinrich, 151
Robert, Paul, 168
Robertson, D. W., 40
Rules of thumb, 18, 59

Sacheverell, Henry, 24
Sainte-Beuve, C. A., 169
Sapir, Edward, 51
Schelling, F. W. J. von, 32
Schemata, 31–34
Schiller, J. C. F. von, 42, 56
Schleiermacher, F. E. D., 17–19, 43, 76–78, 163
Shumaker, Wayne, 164
Searle, J. R., 26, 68, 71, 159, 162
Shakespeare, William, 88, 107, 134
Shawcross, John (editor of S. T. Coleridge), 164, 168

Shelley, P. B., 89, 121, 141
Sherwood, Mary Martha, 169
Sidney, Sir Philip, 121
Significance. See Meaning
Sincerity as a literary criterion, 117
Skepticism in humanistic study, 4, 45, 123, 141, 147, 153
Snell, Bruno, 39, 40, 160
Sociology of knowledge, 147, 152
Sophocles, 107, 118
Sotheby, William, 164
Speech-act theory, 26–27, 34, 68
Spiegelberg, Herbert, 159
Spitzer, Leo, 162
Staiger, Emil, 129
Stein, Gertrude, 55
Stern, H., 161
Stevenson, Charles, 90
Stipulative definition, 59
Strawson, P. F., 68–69, 71, 160, 162
Stylistics, 10, 22, 23, 25; and synonymity, 50–73
Subjective stance, 101–4, 106–8
Sutton, Walter, 167
Swift, Jonathan, 80
Synonymity, 10, 22, 50–73, 149, 161
Synthetic judgment (in logic), 55

Tautology, 54–55, 58
Tension as literary criterion, 121
Textual editing, 89
Tolstoy, Leo, 105, 115, 122, 130, 131
Tragedy, 138
Trilling, Lionel, 166
Types, concepts of, 33, 35

Un-birthday presents, 51
Universal subjective validity, 99–100, 103, 105
University study of literature, 136

Validation in interpretation, 33, 45, 108, 147
Valuation, 95–170
Value, 78, 85, 157; correlation with knowledge, 146–58; correlation with meaning, 11, 95–109; relational theory of, 97–98
Vergil, 76–77
*Verstehen* contrasted with *erklären*, 150
Vico, Giambattista, 41, 160
Visual perception as cognitive model, 30, 47, 48
Voice spectrograph, 64
Voltaire, 132, 168
Vorländer, Karl, 163

Walzel, Oskar, 129
Warnock, G. J., 162

Warren, Austin, 163
Weber, Max, 152
Weimann, Robert, 167
Weitz, Morris, 164
Wellek, René, 11, 97–100, 105–6, 126, 133, 163
*Welt*, 83–84, 147–48
*Weltanschauung*, 42
Whewell, William, 150
Whorf, Benjamin Lee, 51, 161
Wilde, Oscar, 146
Wilson, Edmund, 166
Wimsatt, W. K., 125–26, 129
Windelband, Wilhelm, 150–51
Winters, Yvor, 43, 125, 126, 165
Wittgenstein, Ludwig, 25, 68, 121, 164
Written speech as literature, 90, 130

Ziff, P., 54, 162

I wish I was a seagull flying
High above the sea
Spying out the fishes in their
fishy revelry.
'Cause then I wouldn't have to w[ork]
So hard at being smart.
Instead I'd leave a patterned trail
And you would call it art.